THE
Food Combining
MENU COOKBOOK

THE
Food Combining
MENU COOKBOOK

MEALS FOR A HEALTHY LIFESTYLE

BY SUZANNE GIBBS

INTRODUCED BY TIM SPONG

SALLY MILNER PUBLISHING

First published in 1992 by
Sally Milner Publishing Pty Ltd
67 Glassop Street
Birchgrove NSW 2041 Australia

© Suzanne Gibbs, 1992

Photography by Ray Jarrett
Front cover photograph by Rowan Fotheringham
Design by Gatya Kelly, Doric Order
Production by Sylvana Scannapiego,Island Graphics
Typeset in Australia by Asset Typesetting Pty Ltd
Printed in Australia by Impact Printing, Melbourne

National Library of Australia
Cataloguing-in-Publication data:

Gibbs, Suzanne.
    The food combining menu cookbook.

    ISBN 1 86351 062 1.

    1. Reducing diets – Recipes. 2. Health-Nutritional aspects. I. Title.
    (Series: Milner healthy living guide).

641.5635

Contents

Foreword

Food combining has its critics. Some say it's not scientifically proven. And they are right! There isn't a battery of repeatable experiments that conclusively prove the benefits of eating foods that digest well together at the one meal. But to dismiss food combining on that basis alone is foolhardy.

I say this because literally hundreds of thousands of people world-wide have benefitted from adopting this simple eating pattern. During my work at the Hopewood Health Centre in Sydney, I have personally seen many thousands of people make quite remarkable improvements in their energy levels and adopt easy long-term weight management programs. In particular, I have watched many people with quite significant digestive disorders gain tremendous benefits from simply rearranging the foods they eat.

Surely that is the real test! If we feel so much better as a result of following food combining principles, then there must be something in it. Does it really matter that we do not, at this stage, fully understand all that underlies this eating program?

Food combining is simple once you become familiar with the basic guidelines. It does not require that you avoid certain foods as do most diets, which is probably why so many people don't stick with diets for very long. What food combining suggests is that we rearrange the food we eat into harmonious combinations to assist digestion.

There is nothing magical in food combining that causes people to lose weight. What it does is bring a better overall balance to our eating patterns. With food combining, we tend to eat less starch and protein-rich foods, but we still have both on a daily basis, which is important for our energy needs and for many other functions as well. We also become more aware of what we are eating, the result being we eat more fresh fruit and vegetables without thinking consciously about it.

I suggest you see food combining merely as guidelines, not as a set of rules and regulations. (If you are like me, you would probably dig your heels in and do the opposite.) With food combining, the more you do, the better you'll feel, and that's what keeps you moving forward. Very soon it becomes simply a way of life, not a restrictive diet.

Set yourself easily attainable goals. For example, aim for one meal a week that is properly combined. Then one meal a day. Before you know it, you will be correctly combining all your meals. The beauty of food combining is that you will be gently encouraged to continue because the more you do the better you'll feel.

There is a comment about healthy food I have heard more than once: 'If it's bland and boring, then it's got to be healthy!' In the past there may have been some truth in such a remark, but not today. More than ever we are showing a willingness to change for our health's sake. Where once people enjoyed rich gourmet-style food despite low energy levels, expanded waistlines and perhaps even digestive disorders, they are now taking stock.

That is why it is wonderful that such a well-known cookery writer such as Suzanne Gibbs has applied her creative talents to a wide selection of popular recipes based on food combining principles. This cookbook fills a huge void and will attract anyone taking the first steps towards adopting an improved eating program. The arrangement of recipes into menus is a brilliant stroke, for it makes the selection of food so much easier. It is also ideal for those situations when you need to prepare meals for people who haven't yet taken those first steps. All they will know is that they simply loved the meal.

At Hopewood Health Centre we are somewhat stricter in the way we apply the principles of food combining. With the needs of our guests to consider, we have to be. Food combining is not black and white and that is why most people will be able to tolerate minor inconsistencies in the application of these principles. For example, a very small amount of protein in a starch meal will not cause problems for most people and they will still gain many benefits.

Finally, I would encourage you to see food combining as part of your overall improved lifestyle. An equally important aspect is exercise. Find some form of exercise you enjoy and do it regularly. The management of stress is also important. You can eat all the best foods in the world in correct combinations, but if you are racked by stress, your digestion will be severely affected. And don't forget to explore the spiritual side of your life by following whatever direction you are attracted to.

Remember you are a whole person and the real key to long-term good health and vitality involves drawing all these aspects together.

Tim Spong
General Manager
Hopewood Health Centre

Introduction

I was recently introduced to food combining during a stay at Hopewood Health Centre at Wallacia, near Sydney. After a regime of carefully planned meals based on food combining principles I emerged a new woman. I came away feeling fresher, brighter and more energetic and, best of all, clear-headed.

It took little persuasion for me to accept the challenge to write a book of recipes using the basic principles of food combining. The rewards of food combining were clearly evident.

Today it has never been easier to eat well and take care of our health at the same time. Food writers, nutritionists and producers of foods have all played their part in changing our eating habits for the better.

Food combining is an eating program, not a diet. It's a method of combining foods which asks that we take a second look at what we eat and the way we eat it. It's guidelines are basic common sense, based on the principle that better digestion promotes easier health.

If you are overweight, food combining will help you lose weight painlessly. If you are just right, then it will assist you to maintain your proper weight. Best of all, you'll feel good! It can also help you put on weight if you need to through better assimilation of nutrients.

The aim of this book is to enable you to enjoy food combining. As a food writer, I am often asked what kind of food I like best. I was instructed in the French classical method, but I love the simple freshness of Asian cooking and Middle Eastern cooking intrigues me. I have travelled widely and am familiar with the food of many countries. There are, for me, few pleasures greater than cooking and eating good food from all over the world and it can all fit within a food combining regime.

Food combining, put simply, is the art of eating good food in combinations which harmonise. Food combiners believe, for example, that digestion and the absorption of essential nutrients are improved by not mixing proteins with starches in the one meal. At the same time a great deal of importance is laid on which fruits combine best with either food group.

The charts shown on the next pages clearly sets out which foods can be eaten with what fruits and other foods. For more detailed information please refer to Tim Spong and Vicki Peterson's book *Food Combining for Dynamic Energy, Weight Loss and Vitality at Any Age*.

I have written this book as a menu cookbook rather than a recipe cookbook to help you follow a food combining program at home. There is little gained in combining a single dish skilfully, then wrongly combining the rest of the meal. A planned menu allows the food combiner to go ahead and prepare a meal with confidence. At a glance you will see what kinds of dishes can be cooked and combined in one meal.

Once you begin food combining as a way of eating you will find that you never feel deprived as you do on a diet. No ingredients are forbidden or considered bad for your health, although some are best eaten in moderation. It is the way they are put together that makes the difference. These recipes have been designed to fit in with today's lighter, healthier approach to eating.

Most important of all, cooking, menu-planning, entertaining and keeping a good table should always be a pleasurable occupation. Working with fresh, colourful, fragrant ingredients, transforming them into flavourful dishes and taking the greatest possible care of your health, and that of the people you love, makes for a happy life.

FOOD COMBINATIONS

Read down the first column and then across for the combination.

	Protein	Starch	Fats/ Oils	Vege- tables	Sweet Fruits	Sub-Acid Fruits	Acid Fruits
Protein	Yes	No	Yes*	Yes	No	Yes*	Yes
Starch	No	Yes	Yes*	Yes	Yes	Yes*	No
Fats/Oils	Yes*	Yes*	Yes*	Yes*	Yes*	Yes*	Yes*
Vegetables	Yes	Yes	Yes*	Yes	Yes	Yes	Yes
Sweet Fruits	No	Yes	Yes*	Yes	Yes	Yes	No
Sub-Acid Fruits	Yes*	Yes*	Yes*	Yes	Yes*	Yes	Yes
Acid Fruits	Yes	No	Yes*	Yes	No	Yes	Yes

*denotes combinations to be used only in moderation.

The Food Combining Menu Cookbook

FOOD LIST (example foods only)

Fats/Oils
Avocados
Oils
Macadamia Nuts
Pecan Nuts
Coconut
Olives

Acid Fruits
Grapefruit
Lemon
Oranges
Lime
Mandarin
Pineapple
Strawberry
Kiwi Fruit
Gooseberry
Passionfruit

Starch
Rice
Wheat
Corn
Rye
Millet
Buckwheat
Lima Beans
Red Beans
Pinto Beans
Nary Beans
Mung Beans
Broad Beans
Garbanzoes
Lentils
Chestnuts
Breadfruit
Jackfruit
Potato
Sweet Potato
Jerusalem Potatoes
Pumpkins
Taro
Yams

Protein
Primary:
Almonds
Brazil Nuts
Cashew Nuts
Hazel Nuts
Pine Nuts
Pistachios
Walnuts
Pepitas
Sunflower seeds
Sesame seeds
Wheat germ
Lecithin
Soyabean
Secondary:
Peanuts
Cheese
Eggs
Yogurt
Poultry
Meat
Fish

Sub-Acid Fruits
Mulberry
Raspberry
Blackberry
Blueberry
Grapes
Pears
Apples
Cherries
Apricots
Peaches
Plums
Nectarines
Pawpaws
Mangoes
Guava

Melons
Cantelopes
Watermelon
Honeydew

Sweet Fruits
Bananas
Figs
Custard Apples
Monsteria Deliciosa
Persimmon
All dried fruits

Vegetables
Globe Artichokes
Fresh Sprouts
Beetroot
Carrot
Capsicum
Cucumber
Swedes
Parsley
Brussels Sprouts
Cauliflower
Cabbage
Celery
Lettuce
Turnips
Beans
Peas
Zucchini
Chokoes
Marrows
Squash
Broccoli
Asparagus
Egg Plant
Silver Beet
Spinach
Tomatoes
   (not with starches)
Onions (best cooked)

Table 2

11

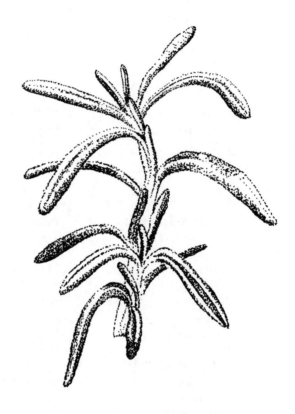

Breakfast — Start the Day right

Everyone agrees that people who have a good breakfast are more efficient, more productive and noticeably better tempered than those who make do with toast and coffee gulped down with unseemly haste.

Most of us lead busy lives. School children catch early transport to get to school on time. Blue and white collar workers often have several changes of transport. Let's face it, staying in bed for those extra minutes seems very attractive. But leave yourself time to enjoy a breakfast and you will be really set up for the day.

First you can prepare a basic muesli. It is important to add at least one piece of fruit when serving it. A freshly grated apple, skin and all, is a favourite. Each day on rising, enjoy lemon or grapefruit juice with hot or cold water, or have a glass of pure apple juice.

Easily digested, light and energy giving, fruit is a happy choice for breakfast, especially in a country where a great variety of fruits are available throughout the year. Eaten singly or in fruit salads or as a salad plate, fruit is always a welcome sight. Try these suggestions.

Fruit Combinations

APPLE AND NUTS
Coarsely grated unpeeled apple, sprinkled with lemon juice and combined with 1 tablespoon chopped nuts or skim milk yogurt.

SUMMER FRUIT SALAD
Chunks of peach, apricot and plum, sprinkled with a little lemon juice.

FRUITS WITH YOGURT
Try fresh or poached fruit with natural low fat yogurt. Yogurt with fresh orange segments is a good combination.

CUBES OF FRESH PAWPAW
These can be sprinkled with a little lemon juice.

DRIED FRUIT SALAD
Soak the fruit in water for a few hours, or overnight. Cook until just tender. Delicious served either warm or at room temperature, by itself or with yogurt. Dried pears, peaches, nectarines, apricots, plums (prunes) can be used singly or in combination.

FRESH ROCKMELON
Diced or in wedges, this makes a refreshing start to the day. A fine sprinkling of ground ginger gives it a lift. You can use honeydew melon in the same way.

Melons are best eaten alone or at least half an hour before the main course. That's if you plan to serve them as an appetiser. Melons digest extremely quickly and can ferment if forced to sit on other slower digesting foods.

Pep Drinks

These are excellent for those who fly out of bed to the door in the morning. These can almost be drunk on the run and should keep a person vital until lunch time.

QUICK PEP JUICE

1 fresh egg yolk
1 cup unsweetened orange juice

In a blender or food processor beat the egg yolk into orange juice until frothy. Drink immediately.

FRUIT-NUT MILK

¼ cup nuts (almonds, pecans or walnuts)
1 cup fruit juice

Place nuts in an electric blender or food processor and grind finely. Add fruit juice and honey and blend together for about 30 seconds until smooth.

Breakfast in a Glass

1 egg
1 cup orange juice
1 tablespoon lemon juice
1 tablespoon wheatgerm

Put all the ingredients into a blender and blend at high speed for 30 seconds.

Yogurt Smoothies

1 wedge of fresh pineapple
1 thin slice lemon
⅔ cup low fat yogurt

Put all the ingredients together in a blender and blend at high speed for 60 seconds. Strawberries, raspberries, fresh peaches, apricots or plums, washed and sliced, may replace the pineapple.

Hopewood Muesli

Rice is one of the most easily digested foods. For this reason rice flakes are used in place of oats at Hopewood Health Centre.

1 tablespoon rice flakes
1 tablespoon shredded coconut (optional)
1 tablespoon sultanas or raisins
pinch cinnamon
1½ cups chopped fresh fruit (apples, grapes, etc.)
¼ cup apple or grape juice

Soak rice flakes in apple or grape juice for at least 1 hour or overnight if possible. Add remainder of ingredients and mix.

Bircher Muesli

3 tablespoons oatmeal
3 tablespoons water
1 apple
honey to taste

Soak the oats in the water overnight. In the morning, wash the apple and grate into the oats without peeling it. Stir lightly and serve at once with the honey. A spoonful of natural low-fat yogurt can be served with this.

Treat yourself to a fruit-based meal every few days. That is, breakfast of fruit as well as an evening fruit-based meal. It will help digestion, increase energy levels, promote internal cleansing and help control any weight problems.

The Food Combining Menu Cookbook

Salad Meals

Whatever the season, nothing tempts the appetite like a beautiful salad. The availability of wonderful fresh vegetables and fruits gives so much scope for creating new combinations, and nothing could be healthier.

Main course salads are becoming more and more popular as people consider their health and well-being. In order to make a nutritious and satisfying main course the food combiner has to learn to make protein salads and starch salads using the abundance of neutral vegetables available to them.

Because salad meals are usually more casual, simple affairs, I have not given menus for using them. You will quickly see which are protein and which are carbohydrate, and the recipes are complete meals.

Remember too that salads make an excellent substitute for the sandwich. I've included a few ideas for packed lunches.

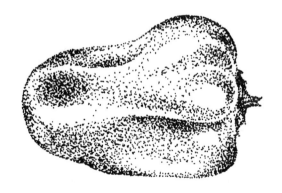

French Rice and Broccoli Salad

Starch

1½ cups raw rice (long grain)
4 cups boiling water
250g (8oz) broccoli florets
1 quantity vinaigrette dressing
  (see below)
1 red pepper, cut into thin strips
½ cup chopped parsley
1 cup finely chopped spring onions,
  including green stalks
1 small red onion, diced
salt and freshly ground pepper

VINAIGRETTE
1 tablespoon Dijon mustard
2 tablespoons white wine vinegar
⅓ cup light olive oil
salt and pepper to taste

Wash rice well under cold, running water. Dribble rice slowly into rapidly boiling water. Stir once, then cover and turn the heat very low. Steam for 15 minutes, or until rice is just tender. Remove lid, stand for 2 minutes to let steam escape, then fluff up rice with a fork. Cool to room temperature. Meanwhile drop broccoli into a small pan of boiling water. Cook for 3 minutes, drain and refresh under cold water. Cool and mix with rice and dressing, adding red pepper strips, parsley, chopped spring onions and red onion. Season with salt and freshly ground pepper, if necessary, and toss well.

VINAIGRETTE DRESSING: In a small bowl whisk mustard with vinegar. Gradually whisk in olive oil until dressing is emulsified. Add salt and pepper to taste.

Serves 4

Remember it is what we eat 95 per cent of the time that counts, not a 5 per cent slip up. So don't feel bad if you make mistakes and combine the wrong courses. Just try again.

Chef's Salad

Protein

A chef's salad is one made by the chef using whatever is fresh and on hand. Like a nicoise salad in France, the ingredients depend on the season and region. Two features that all chef's salads should share are that at least two of the ingredients are cut into matchstick strips (such as the ham and cheese) and that it be made with the freshest of ingredients.

A chef's salad is often as expected, but if you discard the idea of making it with odds and ends, and julienne the ingredients beautifully, it can be spectacular. This version of a chef's salad is made with a blue cheese dressing.

1 bunch English spinach, washed, trimmed and patted dry
1 telegraph cucumber, thinly peeled and sliced across
¼ cup finely sliced green shallots
125g (4oz) ham or salami, cut into thin strips
100g (3oz) cheese, either havarti, gruyère, emmenthaler or other cheese of good quality, cut into thin strips
3 hard-boiled eggs, quartered
freshly ground pepper to taste

BLUE CHEESE DRESSING
3 tablespoons wine vinegar
salt and freshly ground pepper
⅓ cup olive oil
1 tablespoon thick cream
2-3 tablespoons crumbled blue cheese
a few drops of lemon juice

In a large bowl, toss the spinach leaves which have been torn into large, bite-size pieces, the sliced cucumber, and half the shallots with half the mixed Blue Cheese Dressing. Divide among 4 or 6 individual salad bowls and arrange the salami and cheese and egg quarters over. Sprinkle with the remaining shallots and drizzle with the remaining dressing.

BLUE CHEESE DRESSING: To make the dressing combine the vinegar in a bowl with the salt and pepper to taste. Whisk in the oil and cream in a thin stream until the dressing is emulsified. Stir in the blue cheese and lemon juice.

Serves 4-6

Potato and Watercress Salad

Starch

1kg (2lb) potatoes
1 bunch watercress
a few fresh basil leaves
1 clove garlic
1 teaspoon french mustard
1 tablespoon tarragon vinegar

¼ cup dry white wine
1 teaspoon salt
freshly ground pepper
½ cup light olive oil
2 cups sliced celery

If using tiny new potatoes, scrape skins with a small sharp knife, plunge them into boiling salted water and cook until tender. If using large, older potatoes, cover with cold salted water, bring to the boil and cook until tender. Drain and peel. Slice potatoes fairly thickly.

Pick over watercress, discarding tough stalks and yellowing leaves. In a blender or food processor, process a cup of watercress leaves, basil leaves, garlic, mustard, vinegar and wine until leaves are finely chopped. Add salt and pepper and, with the motor still running, add the oil gradually until a thick dressing is made.

Toss the potatoes in the dressing while they are still warm then cool to room temperature. Line a salad platter with the remaining watercress. Arrange a ring of sliced celery 2cm (1 inch) from the edge. Pile the dressed potatoes over the watercress and inside the sliced celery to serve.

Serves 4-6

Bacon, Avocado and Tomato Salad

Protein

A lovely first course salad or light luncheon dish.

lettuce leaves, preferably butterhead
  or mignonette
2 firm red tomatoes
salt and freshly ground pepper
1 tablespoon finely chopped salad
  onion

1 tablespoon olive oil
1 ripe avocado
3 rashers bacon, rind removed and
  cut across into 2cm (1 inch) strips

Wash lettuce leaves and dry well and arrange on 2 dinner plates. Slice tomatoes and arrange, overlapping, along the edge of the lettuce. Season well with salt and pepper and sprinkle tomato with onion and oil.

Peel, halve and stone avocado and cut each half lengthwise into crescent-shaped slices. Arrange the slices overlapping alongside the tomato.

When ready to serve, fry the bacon in a dry frying pan over a high heat, turning until lightly browned. Pour the hot bacon and drippings over the avocado and serve immediately.

Serves 2

Sandwiches and fillings pose a problem for good food combining. How about changing over to salads if you want protein fillings. Try grated vegetables and avocado with bread.

Mediterranean Chicken Salad

Protein

1 size 18 chicken (4lb) *or* 4 whole
  chicken breasts
2 large onions, quartered
2 stalks celery
salt and whole peppercorns
¼ cup olive oil
1 teaspoon fresh oregano leaves
a selection of salad greens (e.g.
  mignonette, butterhead lettuces,
  watercress and arugula)

2 red peppers, charred, skinned,
  seeded and shredded
¼ cup black olives, halved and pitted
2 tablespoons capers
250g (8oz) fresh green beans,
  cooked
juice of 1 lemon
salt and freshly ground pepper to
  taste

Put the whole chicken into a large pan (the breasts can be cooked in a smaller pan), cover with water, onions, celery, salt and peppercorns. Bring slowly to the boil, cover and simmer gently for about 1 hour for whole chicken, 15 minutes for breasts, or until just tender. Leave chicken to cool in liquid. Drain the chicken, reserving the stock for another dish, and remove the skin. Pull the flesh from the bones and shred into bite-size pieces. Combine in a bowl with the olive oil and oregano. Cover and marinate for at least an hour.

Arrange salad greens on a serving platter and top with marinated chicken. Garnish the platter with the remaining ingredients and season to taste with the lemon juice, salt and a good grinding of pepper.

Serves 6

If food combining requires that you think more about what you are eating, then good. We need to pay closer attention to the food we eat for our health's sake.

The Food Combining Menu Cookbook

American Potato Salad

Starch

To make a very special warm potato salad splash the still-hot potatoes with dry white wine or vermouth as done here.

1kg (2lbs) new potatoes
salted water
$\frac{1}{3}$ cup dry white wine
½ cup vinaigrette dressing
  (see page 18)
1 red onion, sliced into rings
1 stalk celery, sliced
2 dill pickles or gherkins, thinly
  sliced

1 teaspoon capers
chopped parsley
salt and freshly ground pepper
a selection of salad greens
  (e.g. mignonette, butterhead
  lettuces, watercress and arugula)

Scrub and boil potatoes until tender in salted water. While still hot peel and slice them into a bowl. Sprinkle with white wine, turning the potato slices carefully. Now sprinkle with the vinaigrette dressing and add the remaining ingredients. Season with salt and pepper. Serve accompanied with a bowl of a selection of salad greens.

Serves 6

Avoid drinking hot drinks for at least an hour after a meal. (That includes that after dinner coffee.) Heat can affect and slow down digestion considerably.

Salad Meals

Confetti Rice with Two Basils

Starch

Avoid shredding the basil until the last moment.

1 cup raw brown rice
2 tablespoons white vinegar
1 teaspoon balsamic vinegar
salt to taste
plenty of freshly ground pepper
⅓ cup olive oil
6 green shallots, finely chopped
2 tablespoons each finely shredded
  green and purple basil
  (when available)

2 tablespoons chopped parsley
2 stalks celery, finely chopped
1 red pepper, finely diced
2 ears fresh young sweet corn,
  cooked and kernels cut off *or* 1 cup
  canned corn kernels, drained
½ to 1 cup sprouted beans

Wash rice, place in saucepan with 3 cups water, bring to the boil, reduce heat, cover and cook gently for 15-20 minutes or until tender. Leave to cool in pot. Gently spoon into serving bowl when cooled. Shake vinegars, oil, salt and pepper together in a small bowl and pour over rice. Add remaining ingredients and fold together.

TO COOK CORN: Strip husks and silk from corn, drop into saucepan of boiling unsalted water and simmer 8 minutes. Remove and cut off kernels when cool. Or, cut tops and bottoms from corn, place with husks in microwave and cook high for 4-6 minutes, then stand for 2 minutes. Remove husks and strip silk off.

Serves 6

Noodle Salad with Bean Sprouts

Starch

Somen is a Japanese noodle and is good in salads. Get the crunchy mung bean shoots for this salad. The radish could be daikon, the long white Japanese radish if it is available.

2 tablespoons rice vinegar
2 tablespoons light soy sauce
3 tablespoons peanut oil
1 teaspoon honey
½ pound somen (fine, white, wheat noodles)*

1 carton mung bean shoots
1 carrot, peeled and cut into thin strips with a vegetable peeler
½ cup finely sliced radishes, or if using daikon, cut into thin strips
3 green shallots sliced on the bias

In a blender blend the rice vinegar, soy sauce, oil and honey until the dressing is emulsified.

In a pan of boiling water boil the somen for 2 minutes, or until tender, and drain in a colander. Rinse the somen well under cold water and drain it again. In a salad bowl toss the somen well with the dressing. Add to the noodles the bean shoots, carrot, radish and half the shallots. Toss the mixture gently, and season it with the additional soy sauce. Sprinkle the salad with the remaining shallots.

*available at Oriental markets, specialty food shops, and some supermarkets

Serves 4

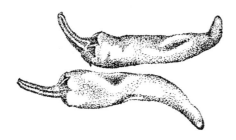

Crunchy Bean Sprout, Lentil and Rice Salad

Starch

Crunchy sprouts, lentil and rice salad, fragrant with cumin and balsamic vinegar.

1 cup dried brown lentils
1 cup long grain rice, boiled and drained
1½ cups mung bean sprouts
½ cup roughly chopped mint leaves
1 small red or salad onion, finely chopped

4 tablespoons olive oil
2 tablespoons balsamic vinegar
1 teaspoon lightly toasted ground cumin
a little salt to taste
freshly ground pepper

Bring a pan of salted water to the boil and cook the lentils until tender, but with still a little crispness, about 30 minutes. Drain and rinse under cold water. Drain thoroughly.

Add lentils to a salad bowl with remaining ingredients and toss very well. Cover and leave in refrigerator for a few hours for the flavours to develop. Garnish with a little freshly chopped mint.

Serves 4-6

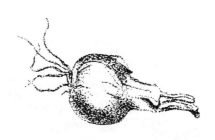

Mussel Salad with Celery

Protein

A lovely, summery lunch, or a light main course for four. Serve on a bed of salad greens.

2.5kg (3lb) mussels, cleaned
1 onion, sliced
6 parsley stalks
pinch crushed peppercorns
1 cup water
1 small head crisp white celery, finely sliced

MUSTARD SAUCE
1 teaspoon dry mustard
juice of ½ small lemon
¼ cup each light sour cream and low fat yogurt
salt and freshly ground black pepper
a selection of salad greens such as mignonette and butterhead lettuce, watercress and arugula
lemon wedges

Place the mussels in a deep pan with the onion, parsley stalks, crushed peppercorns and water, then cover and cook at high heat for 5-7 minutes or until the shells have opened. Remove the mussels from the shells and pull away weed still attached.

MUSTARD SAUCE: Mix the mustard and lemon juice in a bowl then add the sour cream and yogurt, blending together thoroughly. Season with salt and plenty of freshly ground pepper.

Place the cooked mussels in a bowl with the finely sliced celery and lightly fold through the prepared sauce. Arrange on a platter on a selection of salad greens and garnish with lemon wedges.

Serves 4

If you are being entertained and don't want to make a fuss about food combining, do what Sir John Mills the actor suggests: eat the meat and salad; leave the bread roll, ignore the dessert and ask your hostess for cheese and raw vegetables instead.

Prawns with Basil

Protein

If you live near fish markets or a good fish shop you will be able to get wonderfully fresh green (raw) prawns. Use them with fresh basil leaves and a good quality olive oil for this salad.

500g (1lb) raw prawns	salt and freshly ground pepper
¼-½ cup light olive oil	1 butterhead or mignonette lettuce
½ cup shredded basil leaves	8 cherry tomatoes
2 tablespoons Pernod or dry vermouth	8-10 arugula leaves, watercress or other greens
squeeze lemon juice	4 lemon wedges

Shell and devein prawns leaving the tail end intact and butterfly along the outer curve, removing the sandy tract or vein. Heat oil in frying pan, add the prawns and basil leaves and sauté until prawns start to turn pink, about 1-2 minutes. Add Pernod and lemon juice and heat through. Transfer to a bowl, season with salt and freshly ground pepper. Allow to cool, chill if liked.

Arrange washed, chilled lettuce leaves on 4 plates, top with halved cherry tomatoes and torn arugula leaves or watercress. Divide prawns between salad plates, spoon the oil in the bowl over the prawns and garnish with lemon wedges and sprigs of basil.

Serves 4

Fusilli Salad with Arugula

Starch

Pasta salads offer endless variety. Fusilli pasta is shaped like little cork screws but any shape can be used. Arugula or watercress adds a sharp pepper taste and welcome green.

2 teaspoons Dijon mustard
3 tablespoons red wine vinegar
¼ cup light olive oil
1 zucchini, scored lengthwise with the tines of a fork, quartered lengthwise, and cut crosswise into ¼ inch slices
250g (8oz) pasta, fusilli or shells or bows

1 small red pepper, cut into dice
3 tablespoons halved black olives
2 tablespoons chopped fresh parsley leaves
4 cups loosely packed arugula or watercress, coarse stems discarded, washed well and spun dry

In a small bowl whisk together the mustard, the vinegar, and salt to taste, add the oil in a stream, whisking until emulsified. In a saucepan of boiling salted water blanch the zucchini for 1 minute, or until it just begins to turn translucent, drain and refresh in a bowl of ice cold water.

In a large saucepan cook the pasta in boiling salted water for 8 minutes, or until they are al dente, drain and refresh under cold water. Drain the zucchini and the pasta well and in a bowl combine with the pepper, the olives, parsley, three-quarters of the dressing, and salt and pepper to taste. Toss the ingredients well to coat with the dressing. In another bowl toss the arugula with the remaining dressing and divide it and the fusilli between plates.

Serves 4

Parsley has high levels of potassium and iron which is particularly beneficial for women. Use it often as a fresh herb in salads and as a garnish.

The Packed Lunch

If you're following a food combining program, a packed lunch is easier to control than a bought take-away or restaurant meal. With such a variety of good lunch boxes and containers available, salads can be a big part of a lunch box. A frozen drink or frozen brick will keep them cool and fresh. Remember to include a fork.

Here are some ideas:

— Mix ricotta or cottage cheese with chopped fresh pineapple, a few sultanas and a little grated lemon rind. Pack in a plastic container and enjoy with plenty of salad vegetable sticks.

— When grilling steak, grill an extra piece. Cut into strips, pack in a plastic container, and sprinkle with a little teriyaki sauce and finely chopped fresh ginger. Excellent cold for next day's lunch, with radishes and shallots.

— Drain tuna packed in brine and mix with grated carrot, lots of chopped celery, a little chopped onion and a spoonful of mayonnaise. Carry crisp lettuce leaves separately.

— Cold scrambled eggs are delicious. Cook them in a non-stick pan, using just a touch of butter, and add fresh chopped herbs if you have them. Cool, then pack in a plastic container with salad vegetables.

POTATO SALADS: Cook extra potatoes for the evening meal, cut them up and put into a bowl. Sprinkle with a little vinegar or white wine while warm, then toss lightly and cool. Add enough mayonnaise to moisten. For flavour add one or more of the following: chopped gherkin or capers, sliced celery, grated carrot, chopped spring onion and for those who like it, chopped or grated raw beetroot.

RICE SALADS: When cooking rice for the evening meal, add an extra cupful (you will have 3 extra cups cooked rice). Make a salad by moistening rice with vinaigrette or other salad dressing. Add one or more of the following: celery, diced peppers, chopped spring onions, cooked green peas, bean sprouts, chopped parsley or snipped dill or shredded basil leaves and slivered olives. For a creamy salad add a little mayonnaise.

PASTA SALADS: Any type of pasta or noodles are a popular foundation for salads. Cook pasta of choice according to package instructions, drain and rinse with fresh water, then drain again. Moisten noodles or pasta with a little vinaigrette or other dressing. Here are a few suggestions to add: black olives, drained artichokes in oil, capers, sliced celery, chopped herbs, steamed snow peas or broccoli, bean sprouts, little mayonnaise, cooked green peas or broad beans, sliced red or green pepper. For a creamy salad add a little mayonnaise.

Summer Meals

MENU 1 — PROTEIN
(for 6)
Orange, Onion and Cress Salad
Chicken Fillets with Gingered Julienne of Vegetables
or Jewfish with Tomato Coriander Sauce
Pears with Fresh Passionfruit Sauce

MENU 2 — STARCH
(for 6)
Romaine Lettuce with Garlic Croutes
Pasta with Mushroom, Olive and Parsley Sauce
Blueberry Apple Cobbler

MENU 3 — PROTEIN
(for 6-8)
Witloof with Herbed Cheese
or Cucumber Soup with Mint
Grilled Chicken *or* Fish with Tomato Herb Sauce
Arugula and Red Onion Salad
Summer Fruits in Wine

MENU 4 — PROTEIN
(for 6)
Grilled Eggplant with Basil Sauce
Kebab Bang
Minted Oranges in Wine Syrup
Dried Apricot Mousse

Orange, Onion and Cress Salad

If possible, for this colourful combination choose cos or iceberg lettuce which keep their crisp texture on standing.

1 cos lettuce
½ bunch watercress *or* 1 bunch
  arugula
3 large oranges
½ red onion or other salad onion

SALAD DRESSING
¼ teaspoon Dijon mustard
⅓ cup light olive or cold-pressed
  sunflower oil
2 teaspoons lemon juice

Wash lettuce and watercress, drain very well and whirl in a salad spinner or tea towel. Store in a plastic bag in refrigerator until ready to use. Peel oranges, removing all the white pith and thinly slice. Thinly slice onion into half-rings. When ready to serve, tear lettuce into bite-size pieces and watercress into sprigs. Place in salad bowls, scatter with the orange and onion slices and sprinkle with the salad dressing.

SALAD DRESSING: Place the mustard, salt and lemon juice in a screw top jar and shake lightly. When ready to serve, add the oil and shake together in the jar.

Serves 6.

Combine sweet fruits with starches. A nice simple mix is a banana sandwich.

The Food Combining Menu Cookbook

Menu 1

Chicken Fillets with Gingered Julienne of Vegetables

Although this requires last minute cooking, everything can be prepared and ready to cook.

4-6 chicken breast fillets
salt and freshly ground pepper
1 teaspoon ground ginger
15g (½oz) butter
¼ cup green ginger wine *or* white
  wine

GINGERED JULIENNE
250g (4oz) carrots
2 zucchini
2 stalks celery
1 tablespoon olive or cold-pressed
  sunflower oil
½ teaspoon cumin seed
1 tablespoon peeled and grated fresh
  green ginger
1 clove garlic, crushed
½ cup water
1 tablespoon lemon juice

Prepare the chicken breasts and season with a little salt, pepper and ginger. Melt the butter in a large frying pan and, when sizzling, add the chicken pieces. Cook for 4 to 5 minutes on each side. Add the ginger wine and boil briskly until chicken is coated with a syrupy glaze. Arrange on a heated platter with the Gingered Julienne of vegetables and serve.

GINGERED JULIENNE OF VEGETABLES: Cut the carrots, zucchini and celery into thin, 5cm-long strips about the size of matchsticks. If you have a vegetable slicer with a julienne cutting blade use this. In a heavy pan heat the oil and fry the cumin gently until fragrant. Add the ginger, garlic and vegetables and cook, stirring, for 1 minute. Add the water and lemon juice and cook uncovered until liquid has evaporated and vegetables are just tender, about 5 minutes.

Serves 6

Menu 1

Jewfish with Tomato Coriander Sauce

This recipe is also suitable for kingfish, ling, gemfish or sea perch.

4-6 jewfish cutlets or other fish
  fillets
a little salt and freshly ground black
  pepper
juice of ½ lemon
6 spring onions
1 tablespoon light olive or cold-
  pressed sunflower oil

3 ripe tomatoes
1 green pepper
½ cup dry white wine vegetable stock
  or water
¼ cup chopped coriander
coriander sprigs to garnish

Wipe the cutlets with a clean, damp kitchen towel. Season lightly with salt and white pepper and sprinkle with lemon juice. Place in a large well-buttered ovenproof dish.

Finely chop spring onions, sauté in oil until soft without colouring. Meanwhile scald tomatoes with boiling water, skin and chop roughly. Cut pepper in half and remove seeds, cut into strips and put aside. Add tomatoes to onions in pan and cook gently for a few minutes. Draw pan off heat, add the wine or stock, chopped coriander and pepper strips. Heat gently for 2 minutes. Pour sauce over fish, cover with a lid or aluminium foil and bake in a preheated moderately hot oven 190°C (375°F) for about 20 minutes or until fish is cooked. Scatter with coriander sprigs and serve.

Serves 6

Salt is linked to hypertension. As a seasoning, why not try granulated kelp, or even a good vegetable salt.

The Food Combining Menu Cookbook

Menu 1

Pears with Fresh Passionfruit Sauce

A simple dessert with wonderful fresh fruit flavours. Choose firm pears for cooking and take care to cook them until just tender.

30g (1oz) butter
2 tablespoons sugar
4-6 ripe pears, peeled, halved and cored
¾ cup orange juice

1 teaspoon ground ginger
45g (1½oz) butter
6 passionfruit
¼ cup water
2 tablespoons sugar

Melt 15g (½oz) butter in a shallow ovenproof serving dish, just large enough to take the pear halves in one layer. Sprinkle the dish with half the sugar. Cut the pears across into thick slices, not quite through, and arrange cut side down in the dish. Pour over the orange juice, sprinkle with remaining sugar and ginger and top each pear with a tiny piece of butter. Bake uncovered in a preheated very hot oven 225°C (110°F) for 20 minutes, basting several times with cooking juices.

Meanwhile halve the passionfruit and scoop the flesh into a small bowl. In a small heavy pan heat the water and sugar together until sugar is dissolved and a light syrup is formed. Stir the syrup into the passionfruit pulp.

Arrange pear halves on serving plates and spoon the juices, then the passionfruit sauce over.

Serves 6

Sugar is a sweetener that should be used in moderation. Because it is empty calories. Try substituting alternatives such as fruit juice concentrates e.g. pear, apple or blackcurrant. But don't over do it.

Menu 2

Romaine Lettuce with Garlic Croutes

1 small head cos (romaine) lettuce	2 teaspoons Dijon mustard
4 thin slices french bread	salt and freshly ground pepper
3 tablespoons olive oil	2 teaspoons red wine vinegar
2 cloves garlic, peeled but left whole	¼ cup olive oil

Pull the leaves of the lettuce apart and rinse well. Pat dry and store in plastic bag in refrigerator until ready to serve salad.

Halve the slices of bread, leaving on crusts. Heat the oil in a frypan, and when hot add the bread and garlic cloves. Cook, shaking the frypan and turning, until the croutes of bread are golden brown. Drain on crumpled kitchen paper. Discard the garlic cloves, or not, as desired. Cut or tear the lettuce leaves into bite-sized pieces, leave small leaves whole. Put the leaves in a salad bowl and sprinkle with croutes. Put the mustard in a small mixing bowl with a very little salt and pepper to taste. Add the vinegar and beat with a wire whisk. Add the oil, beating briskly until dressing is thickened. Pour the dressing over the salad and toss.

Serves 6

The Food Combining Menu Cookbook

Menu 2

Pasta with Mushroom, Olive and Parsley Sauce

500g (1lb) fresh mushrooms
about ⅓ cup light olive or cold-
  pressed sunflower oil
2 large onions, finely chopped
1 large clove garlic, finely chopped

salt and freshly ground black pepper
⅓ cup dry white wine
¼ cup slivered black olives
6 tablespoons chopped parsley
500g (1lb) pasta

Remove stalks from mushrooms unless using tiny buttons, and cut into thin slices. If mushrooms are large, cut into halves before slicing. Sauté the onion in half the oil until soft and transparent. Add the garlic and, when very lightly coloured, add the mushrooms and salt and pepper. Stir and cook over a moderate heat until mushrooms are cooked and all their liquid evaporated.

Add the wine, let it bubble briskly for a few minutes then stir in the olives and parsley. Cover the pan and let the sauce bubble gently for 10 minutes or so.

Meanwhile cook the pasta in plenty of boiling water to which a teaspoon of oil has been added until cooked 'to the bite' (al dente). Drain thoroughly and toss with the sauce. Lastly drizzle the remaining olive oil over the pasta, toss well and serve.

Serves 6

Garlic is great to use as a flavour booster. It's also said to be a natural antibiotic, so if you like it, use it regularly.

Menu 2

Blueberry Apple Cobbler

You can buy free flowing frozen blueberries. They are so handy to have in your freezer, easy to measure and with superb flavour.

3 tablespoons cornflour
¼ cup granulated sugar
1 cup blueberries
3 apples, peeled, cored and sliced
1½ cups plain flour

¼ cup firmly packed light brown sugar
1½ teaspoons baking powder
1 teaspoon ground cinnamon
60g (2oz) cold butter cut into bits

In a large bowl stir together the cornflour, sugar and add the blueberries and apples. Toss the mixture until it is combined well and transfer it to a buttered deep-dish pie plate.

In a bowl combine well the flour, the brown sugar, the baking powder, the salt and the cinnamon, add the butter, and, using the fingertips rub the mixture until it resembles coarse breadcrumbs. Add ¼ cup plus 2 tablespoons boiling water and stir the mixture until it just forms a dough. Drop spoonfuls of the dough over the blueberry mixture and bake the cobbler on a baking sheet in the middle of a preheated hot 200°C (400°F) oven for 30 to 40 minutes, or until the topping is golden and cooked through. Serve the cobbler warm.

Serves 6

Sugar can be enjoyed as part of a varied diet but should be kept to a minimum. Those who consume high quantities should remain active to avoid becoming overweight. Raw sugar and brown sugar have traces of vitamins and minerals in amounts too small to give any more nutritional advantages than white sugar.

Menu 3

Witloof with Herbed Cheese

250g (4oz) cottage, cream or
  Neufchatel cheese
2 tablespoons low fat yogurt or light
  sour cream
4 tablespoons snipped chives
4 tablespoons finely chopped
  walnuts
1 tablespoon ground paprika
2 tablespoons grated salad onion
½ teaspoon Dijon mustard
4 heads of witloof

TO FINISH
4 tablespoons finely chopped
  walnuts

Combine all ingredients, except witloof and walnuts for finishing, in bowl
of food processor. Process briefly. Cut off base of witloof, gently break off
leaves, leaving small ones for a salad another time. Spread about 1 teaspoon
of mixture on base of each leaf. Coat cheese in finely chopped walnuts.
Arrange on a salad platter.

Serves 6-8

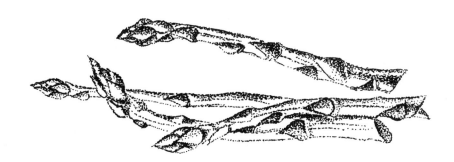

Menu 3

Grilled Chicken

A charcoal barbecue gives poultry a delicious aroma. However, a good oven grill can be used in place of the barbecue.

2 small chickens, split open along the backbone
juice of 1 lemon
½ onion, grated

2-3 cloves garlic, crushed
3 tablespoons olive oil
a little salt and black pepper
¼ teaspoon ground sweet paprika

Prepare the chicken and add with the remaining ingredients to a wide shallow dish. Toss to coat well, cover and leave to marinate for several hours or overnight.

Grill skin side down first over a charcoal fire or under a preheated griller, turning a few times and cooking until golden and tender, about 15 minutes or until the juices run clear when the thickest part of the thigh is pricked.

Serves 6-8

Menu 3

Fish with Tomato and Herb Sauce

Fish is highly prized throughout the Mediterranean. A popular way of cooking whole fish, steaks or cutlets is in fresh tomatoes.

2 garlic cloves, chopped
2 tablespoons olive or cold-pressed sunflower oil
4 medium tomatoes, peeled, deseeded and chopped

a little salt and pepper
1kg (2lb) white fish, whole, steaks or fillets, prepared for cooking
½ cup finely chopped parsley or ¼ cup snipped basil leaves

Gently fry the garlic in the oil in a large pan. Add the tomatoes, salt and pepper and cook for 3 minutes or until the tomatoes have softened. Put the fish in, sprinkle with the parsley and moisten with a little water. Add salt and pepper and simmer gently with a lid on until the fish is done — from 4 minutes for fish steak or fillet to about 15 minutes for a whole fish (head removed). The flesh should just begin to flake from the bone.

Serves 6-8

The Food Combining Menu Cookbook

Menu 3

Arugula and Red Onion Salad

1 mignonette lettuce
1 bunch arugula leaves
1 cup red onion, cut into fine rings
½ cup finely chopped parsley,
 perferably flat-leaf Italian parsley

DRESSING
1 tablespoon red wine vinegar
a little salt and freshly ground
 pepper
¼ cup light olive or cold-pressed
 sunflower oil

Wash lettuce, spin dry and crisp until required. Pick over the arugula leaves and remove and discard any tough stems. Rinse and drain the leaves well. Pat dry. Put the leaves in a salad bowl and add the onion and parsley.

DRESSING: Put vinegar in a bowl and add salt and pepper to taste. Start beating while gradually adding the oil. Pour the dressing over the salad and toss to blend.

Serves 6-8

You will notice arugula is called for throughout this book. It is a herb or salad green with deep green leaves resembling a radish leaf. The taste is quite distinctive with a peppery bite to it. Though it grows easily in a sunny well-drained spot many good green grocers have it for sale these days.

Menu 3

Summer Fruits in Wine

Chilled fruit compotes are one of the simplest and loveliest desserts. One could make this compote of peaches and plums for the colour alone with hardly a thought for the delicious, warmly spiced, wine syrup.

⅓ cup sugar	a strip of orange or lemon rind
1 cup white wine	4 large yellow peaches
2 cups water	4 large red plums
1 cinnamon stick	250g (8oz) stoned cherries
a few whole cloves	¼ cup toasted shredded almonds

Put sugar, wine, water and spices with rind in a heavy saucepan and place over a gentle heat until sugar dissolves. Bring to the boil and simmer for 5 minutes.

Pour boiling water over peaches into a bowl and leave to stand for 3 minutes. Drain and remove the skins. Carefully lower the fruit into the syrup, return to theat and cook gently for 5 to 6 minutes. Remove plum skins if desired. Spoon fruit into a glass bowl and pour over the hot syrup. Cover and allow to cool. Chill in refrigerator.

Serve with a crisp amaretti dessert biscuit.

Serves 6-8

Remember that the alcohol in wine and spirits evaporates when cooked.

Grilled Eggplant with Basil Sauce

2 large eggplants
salt
olive oil
lemon wedges and continental
  parsley or basil to garnish

BASIL SAUCE
3-4 cloves garlic
the leaves of 2 stalks of basil or ½
  cup tightly packed parsley leaves
¼ cup walnuts
2-3 tablespoons light olive or cold-
  pressed sunflower oil

Peel the eggplant and cut into thick slices. Arrange in a colander, sprinkling layers liberally with salt. Leave to drain for about 30 minutes then rinse and pat dry.

Preheat a grill and arrange the eggplant slices on an oiled grilling rack. Brush with oil. Grill, turning once and brushing with oil as they cook until coloured and tender. Keep on a serving dish in a warm place until all are cooked. Serve with the following sauce.

BASIL SAUCE: Using a food processor grind the garlic, basil or parsley and walnuts to a paste then gradually work in the olive oil. Serve with the grilled eggplant slices.

Serves 6

Menu 4

Kebab Bang

This popular Middle Eastern way of barbecuing lamb presents strips of meat threaded onto thin wooden skewers that have been soaked in water overnight.

1.5kg (3lbs) leg of lamb
2 onions, peeled and quartered
1 cup natural, low-fat yogurt

pinch saffron (optional) *or*
  ½ teaspoon ground cumin
a little salt and pepper

Trim all the fat off the lamb. Cut the meat into strips 5cm (2 inches) wide and about 10cm (4 inches) long. Whirl the onions in the blender till soft. Add saffron and yogurt. Put the lamb in a glass, earthenware or stainless steel dish, pour over the yogurt marinade, cover and store in the refrigerator for up to 48 hours. Thread each piece of meat on two thin skewers and grill over hot coals for 3-4 minutes each side. Sprinkle if liked with a little salt and pepper.

Serves 6

Minted Oranges in Wine Syrup

This is the perfect finish to a rich meal, and a useful recipe when you want a make-ahead dessert.

6 large navel oranges
¼ cup sugar
½ cup water
1½ cups dry white wine

4 thin slices lemon peel
1 stick cinnamon
4 cloves
2-3 tablespoons chopped mint

Carefully peel oranges, removing all pith. Cut oranges into slices and arrange decoratively in a glass serving bowl. Combine sugar and water in saucepan, bring to the boil, stirring until sugar is dissolved. Add wine, lemon peel, cinnamon stick and cloves. Bring to the boil and simmer for 15 minutes. Remove from heat, allow to cool a little, then pour over the oranges. Sprinkle with mint and chill, covered, for at least 3 hours.

Serves 6

Dried Apricot Mousse

Simmer dried apricots in a little water to cover to make a purée for this delicious mousse.

1 tablespoon gelatine
1 tablespoon cold water
1 cup purée made from dried
  apricots

3 egg yolks
¼ cup toasted slivered almonds
1½ cups reduced fat cream

Soften gelatine in water, then dissolve over simmering water. Heat purée in a heavy saucepan and stir in gelatine mixture. Beat egg yolks until very light. Add a little of the hot syrup to them, then add remaining syrup mixture, stirring constantly. Cool mixture in the refrigerator for 30 minutes or until the consistency of unbeaten egg whites. Fold in almonds. Whip cream and fold into apricot mixture. Place in a large serving dish or individual serving dishes and chill until set.

A Family Affair

There's nothing like a homemade soup, the aroma of something gently simmering on the stove or baking in the oven to encourage the family to sit down together for a special meal.

MENU 1 — PROTEIN
(for 4-6)
Tomato and Basil Soup
Lamb Stew with Capers
or Sea Perch Baked with Herbs
A Mixed Green Salad
Pears in Apricot Citrus Sauce *or*
Passionfruit Cream

MENU 2 — STARCH
(for 4)
Avocado Dip with Celery Sticks
Pumpkin Stuffed Cabbage Leaves
Apple and Date Crisp

MENU 3 — STARCH
(for 4-6)
Spiced Pumpkin Soup
Mediterranean-Style Stuffed Peppers
A Mixed Green Salad
Autumn Pudding

Tomato and Basil Soup

2 tablespoons light olive or cold-
  pressed sunflower oil
2 large onions, peeled and sliced
1 clove garlic, crushed
1 handful fresh basil, finely snipped
salt and freshly ground pepper,
  to taste

4-6 cups chicken stock
1-1.5kg (2-3lb) tomatoes, coarsely
  chopped
pinch of sugar
grated rind of ½ small lemon
diced cucumber to garnish

Heat oil in a large pan. Add onions and cook gently for 20 minutes or until tender and lightly coloured. Add garlic and cook a further few minutes. Add the basil, season and cook another 15 minutes.

Add chicken stock, tomatoes and sugar. Bring to the boil, reduce heat, cover and simmer for 30 minutes. Push the soup through a sieve. Add lemon rind and salt and pepper to taste. Serve hot or leave to cool. Place in refrigerator to chill for several hours or overnight before serving. Taste and check for seasoning — it may need more after chilling.

Whether serving hot or chilled, ladle the soup into bowls and garnish each with diced cucumber, and, if liked, a thin half-slice of lemon or lime.

Serves 4-6

Soup is a liquid, so drink it half an hour before the meal. And let it cool before you eat it. Hot liquids of all kinds slow down the digestive juices.

Lamb Stew with Capers

A great family dish, full of robust flavours.

1kg (2lb) shoulder lamb
salt and freshly ground pepper
3 tablespoons olive oil
2 medium onions, peeled and
  chopped
1½ cups stock *or* water *or* dry white
  wine

1 sprig of marjoram *or* oregano
2 cloves garlic, crushed
2 green peppers, seeded and diced
1 stalk celery, sliced
2 tablespooons capers
4 tomatoes, peeled and quartered

Trim the lamb of as much fat as possible and cut into fairly large, neat pieces. Season with salt and pepper. Heat the oil in a flameproof casserole and brown the lamb cubes evenly all over. Add the onions and sauté gently until softened. Slowly stir in the stock, water, or wine. Add the marjoram, garlic, peppers and celery. Bring to a simmer, cover and cook over a gentle heat for about 45 minutes. Add the olives and tomatoes and heat through gently.

Serves 4-6

Sea Perch Baked with Herbs

This is a simple way of cooking almost any fish.

4 slices lemon (unpeeled)
4-6 large sea perch fillets
2 tablespoons lemon juice
2 cloves garlic, finely chopped

2 teaspoons chopped fresh herbs
  (parsley, chives and a little thyme)
salt and freshly ground pepper

Place a slice of lemon on each fillet. Mix lemon juice, garlic and herbs. Place fish side by side in a greased baking dish and drizzle herb mixture over them. Season with salt and pepper. Cover dish with foil or a lid and bake in a preheated hot oven 200°C (400°F) for 10 minutes. Uncover, brush with pan juices and bake for a further 3-4 minutes or until fish flakes easily when tested with a fine skewer.

Serves 4-6

Menu 1

Pears in Apricot Citrus Sauce

This is a favourite dessert.

6 large pears, ripe but firm (not hard)
½ cup cooked dried apricot purée
¾ cup water
2 oranges, juiced

rind from 1 orange (peeled with
    vegetable peeler)
juice of 1 lemon

Peel pears, leaving on stalk. Combine remaining ingredients in large saucepan, enamel-lined or stainless steel. Heat gently, add the pears, cover and simmer gently until pears are tender. It will be necessary to turn pears over every now and then, or spoon the syrup over pears during the cooking.

Serve warm or chilled with syrup spooned over. Serve with nut cream if liked.

Serves 4-6

Menu 1

Passionfruit Cream

This may be set in a savarin or ring tin and the centre filled with berry fruits with a little passionfruit squeezed over.

4 eggs, separated
¼ cup sugar
2 cups hot milk

1 envelope (3 teaspoons) gelatine
¼ cup water
pulp of 2 passionfruit

Beat egg yolks, adding sugar gradually, until thick and pale. Stir in hot milk and cook the mixture over a low heat, stirring constantly, until it coats the back of a spoon.

Soften gelatine in water for 5 minutes, dissolve over hot water and stir into custard mixture. Stir in passionfruit. Beat egg whites until they hold soft peaks and fold in custard.

Pour the mixture into a 4-cup mould and chill until firm. Unmould on to a plate and serve plain or with fresh or cooked fruit.

Serves 4-6

The Food Combining Menu Cookbook

Breakfast Fruit Platter (see Breakfasts)

Rice and Broccoli Salad (see Salads)

Chicken Fillets on Gingered Julienne of Vegetables
(see Summer Meals)

Summer Fruits in Wine (see Summer Meals)

Menu 2

Avocado Dip with Celery Sticks

2 avocados, peeled stoned and mashed
1 small spring onion, very finely chopped
1 small clove garlic, crushed

3 tablespoons chopped garlic or coriander
a little lemon juice, salt and pepper to taste
tender celery sticks for serving

Mix ingredients lightly together and chill. Serve with celery sticks for dipping.

Serves 4

For good health it is best to remember that 75 per cent of what we eat each day should be alkaline forming, not acid forming. Meat, grain, tea, coffee and alcohol are acid forming, whereas most fruit and vegetables are alkaline forming. Emphasise the fruits and vegetables and keep acid forming foods to a minimum, you will feel the difference especially if you have rheumatic problems, arthritis, etc.

Pumpkin-Stuffed Cabbage Leaves

This lovely dish of stuffed cabbage leaves with a wonderful fragrance of herbs can be made ahead as it reheats very well.

12 large cabbage leaves
1 medium onion, peeled and
  chopped
1 clove garlic, crushed
1 tablespoon olive oil
375g (12oz) cubed pumpkin, boiled
  or steamed and puréed
4 tablespoons cooked rice or fresh
  breadcrumbs

4 tablespoons chopped parsley
1 teaspoon chopped marjoram
1 tablespoon chopped lovage or
  celery tops
salt and freshly ground pepper
1 cup vegetable stock (see page 119)
extra 2 tablespoons olive oil

Scald the cabbage leaves in a large pan of boiling water. Drain, cool and remove the tough parts. Lay out flat ready for stuffing. Sauté the onion and garlic in the tablespoon of olive oil until softened. Add to a bowl with the pumpkin, rice or breadcrumbs, herbs (only half the parsley) and salt and pepper and mix thoroughly.

Put a large tablespoon of filling on each cabbage leaf, roll a little, tuck in the sides and roll up completely into a small fat sausage, securing with a toothpick. Continue with remaining cabbage leaves, arranging them as you work in a lightly-oiled gratin dish. Top with enough vegetable stock to come two-thirds of the way up the cabbage. Trickle with the extra 2 tablespoons oil.

Cover tightly with foil and bake in a preheated hot oven 220°C (425°F) for 10-15 minutes. Reduce the temperature to slow 150°C (300°F) and continue to bake the cabbage for 1 hour.

Serves 4

Menu 2

Apple and Date Crisp

A great family dessert.

1 cup dates, pitted
½ cup water
1 teaspoon grated lemon rind
¼ cup plus 2 tablespoons sugar
1½ cups self-raising flour

½ teaspoon ground cinnamon
60g (2oz) butter
¾ cup rolled oats
3 large cooking apples, peeled, cored
  and thinly sliced

Combine dates, water, lemon rind and 2 tablespoons sugar in a small pan and cook for 3 minutes or so until dates are very soft. Remove from heat and beat with a wooden spoon until smooth and then allow to cool.

Sift flour and cinnamon into a bowl and rub in the butter which has been cut into small pieces, until mixture resembles coarse breadcrumbs. Stir in remaining sugar and oats. Press about two-thirds of the mixture into a greased and lined 20cm (8 inch) pie dish or square cake tin. Spread with the date mixture. Arrange apple slices over date mixture and top with the remaining oat mixture, pressing down well. Bake in a preheated moderate oven 180°C (350°F) for 45 minutes.

Serves 4

Menu 3

Spiced Pumpkin Soup

Spices and pumpkin. This is a beautiful soup and very satisfying.

1kg (2lb) pumpkin
60g (2oz) butter
1 large onion, chopped
½ teaspoon ground coriander
½ teaspoon ground cumin
a good pinch of grated nutmeg
a little salt and freshly ground
  pepper

1 medium potato, peeled and diced
4 cups vegetable stock or water
a little cream to finish
2 tablespoons chopped coriander or
  parsley

Peel and roughly dice the pumpkin. Put into a pan with the butter, onion, spices and potato. Cover with a lid and simmer over a gentle heat for about 20 minutes. Add the stock or water, bring slowly to the boil and simmer for about 15 minutes, until very tender.

Blend the soup in a blender or food processor or push through a mouli sieve. Reheat gently, adding more vegetable stock or water if necessary to dilute. Check for seasoning and serve with a very little cream floating in each bowl. Scatter coriander or parsley over each serving.

Serves 4-6

Feeling peckish? Celery is the answer here. Celery contains as many kilojoules as it takes to eat it.

Menu 3

Mediterranean-Style Stuffed Peppers

These look spectacular arranged on a large platter. Serve at room temperature as a first course or lunch with crusty bread. They can be made the day before and kept airtight in the refrigerator. They make a delicious family meal, and lend themselves wonderfully to entertaining a crowd.

8 red or green peppers

STUFFING:
¾ cup rice
boiling water
2 onions, chopped
¼ cup olive oil or cold-pressed sunflower oil

1 teaspoon salt
½ cup boiling water
¼ cup currants
¼ teaspoon each ground pepper and allspice
2 tablespoons chopped mint

In a large bowl cover rice with boiling water and stand until water cools to room temperature. Drain and rinse with cold water. Drain again thoroughly.

Meanwhile chop onions and cook in olive oil until pale golden. Add drained rice and continue to stir until rice is pale golden, about 5 minutes. Add boiling water, currants, pepper, allspice, mint and dill. Reduce heat and cook a further 15 minutes until liquid is completely absorbed. Allow to cool completely.

Halve peppers, remove seeds. Fill with stuffing, without packing tightly. Arrange close together in a wide, heavy pan, season with a very little salt and drizzle with 1 tablespoon olive oil. Pour over ½ cup boiling water, cover and simmer 25-30 minutes or until rice and peppers are tender. Add more water if necessary to avoid burning. Cool in pan.

Serves 4-6

A sensible exercise program is vital to good health and maintaining energy levels.

Menu 3

Autumn Pudding

In most areas of Australia blackberries are no longer gathered on roadsides and waste lands. However, thanks to our orchardists, blackberries are now available in punnets at many greengrocers. They are also available frozen, in free-flowing form at many large food halls and supermarkets.

Blackberries ripen later than other berries and should be quite black in colour. Remember to use them as soon as possible after purchase. Here is a variation of the lovely English summer pudding.

2 large cooking apples
500g (1lb) blackberries
about ⅓ cup sugar
8-10 slices sandwich bread

Peel and core the apples and slice them thinly. Place in a saucepan with water to cover and simmer until tender. Add the blackberries and continue to cook until they are soft. Add the sugar and cook until the fruit is pulpy. Strain off the liquid and reserve and rub the fruit through a coarse sieve.

Remove the crusts from the bread and cut each slice into 4 triangles. Arrange triangles first around the edge of the base of a soufflé dish or charlotte mould and then into the centre to cover base of mould. Spoon enough of the fruit purée to just cover the bread. Continue this way, layering the bread and fruit purée, finishing with a bread layer. Cover the top with plastic and then a plate and put a light weight on top. Leave overnight in the refrigerator. The next day turn out on to a serving plate and pour over the reserved juice. Serve cut into wedges with a very little cream.

Serves 4-6

An International Menu

The more we travel the more we accept a new fresh pattern of what makes a good menu. One menu here combines French, Moroccan and Danish specialities to make a starch-based meal, while dishes from Italy and France provide two protein meals.

MENU 1 — STARCH
(for 6)
Green Salad with Garlic Croutons
Couscous with Vegetables
Danish Applecake

MENU 2 — PROTEIN
(for 6)
Salad of Eggplant and Tomatoes
Navarin of Lamb with Baby Vegetables
Biscuit Tortoni with Fresh Fruit

MENU 3 — PROTEIN
(for 6)
Tomato Bocconcini Platter
Tian of Lamb
Arugula Salad
Pineapple and Orange Caramel

Menu 1

Green Salad with Garlic Croutons

This salad has flavour and crunch and looks great. Add croutons just before serving. Prepare croutons, dressing and greens ahead, store in plastic bags and jars and combine just before required. Use 2 bags prepared mesclun in place of the following salad green if wished.

½ bunch watercress
½ bunch Italian parsley
1 frilly green lettuce
1 bunch chives
1 avocado

DRESSING:
¼ cup white wine vinegar
1 teaspoon grain mustard
1 small clove garlic, crushed
¼ cup light olive oil

CROUTONS:
1 cup stale bread cubes cut 1cm x
  1cm (½ inch x ½ inch)
4 tablespoons cold-pressed
  sunflower oil
2 garlic cloves, crushed

Wash the salad greens. Pick leafy sprigs from watercress and parsley and tear lettuce into bite-sized pieces. Pat dry with tea-towel. Snip chives into small bowl. Peel and slice avocados crosswise, dip them in dressing to prevent browning.

Place watercress, parsley, lettuce, three-quarters of the chives, avocados and croutons in serving bowl. Drizzle with dressing, decorate with remaining chives and toss the salad lightly.

CROUTONS: Heat oil in a frying pan over moderate heat. Add bread cubes and fry, tossing constantly for a few minutes until pale golden. Add garlic and continue to cook a minute or so while tossing until croutons are golden brown. Drain on absorbent paper.

DRESSING: Put vinegar, mustard, sugar, garlic and oil in screw-top jar. Shake vigorously to combine.

Serves 6

The Food Combining Menu Cookbook

Menu 1

Couscous with Vegetables

Couscous, a cereal dish originating in North Africa consists of fine semolina combined with flour, salt and water into tiny pellets. It is available at most good health food stores. Try experimenting with different vegetables as they come into season.

500g (1lb) couscous grains
1 small eggplant, diced
75g (2½oz) butter
2 cloves garlic, crushed
½ teaspoon salt
1 teaspoon ground cumin
freshly ground black pepper
½ teaspoon ground ginger
1 bay leaf

1-2 fresh red chillies
4 medium carrots, scraped, cut into
    quarters lengthwise then across into
    5cm (2 inch) lengths
4 zucchini, cut the same size as
    carrots
500g (1lb) potatoes, peeled and cut
    into 5cm (2 inch) lengths
water

Cover couscous with cold water, stir with the fingers and drain. Stand 15 minutes to allow couscous to swell. Repeat this process once more. Salt eggplant, leave to stand 1 hour, rinse off salt and pat dry.

Meanwhile melt 60g (2oz) of the butter in a large heavy saucepan, add the garlic and eggplant and sauté for 1-2 minutes until softened. Add salt, cumin, black pepper, ginger, bay leaf and stir well. Add the whole chillies, vegetables including potatoes, and just enough water to cover and bring to the boil.

Place the swollen couscous in a colander lined with a fine tea towel which will fit snugly into the top of the pan. Place over the vegetables, cover well and simmer gently for about 40 minutes. The couscous grains should not touch the liquid. After 20 minutes add the remaining butter to the couscous. Fluff up the couscous occasionally with a fork during cooking.

To serve, pile the couscous on to a large serving platter, make a well in the centre and pile the vegetables into the centre, removing chillies.

Serves 6

Menu 1

Danish Applecake

The distinctive taste of rye or pumpernickel adds a unique taste to apple purée.

3 tablespoons unsalted butter
125g (4oz) pumpernickel or rye
  breadcrumbs
⅓ cup brown sugar
750g (1½lb) cooking apples

juice of 1 lemon
⅓ cup water
sugar to taste
⅓ cup redcurrant jelly

Melt 2 tablespoons of the butter in a pan, add breadcrumbs and brown sugar and cook, stirring constantly until crisp. Cool.

Peel, core and slice apples and cook with lemon juice and water over a gentle heat until very soft. Mash with a fork and stir in remaining butter with sugar to taste. Cool.

In a glass bowl, arrange alternate layers of the crumbs and apple purée, beginning and ending with the crumbs. Drizzle decoratively with the slightly warmed reducurrant jelly.

Serves 6

Try to rest after a heavy meal. Wait half an hour and then take a gentle stroll. Both promote good digestion.

The Food Combining Menu Cookbook

Salad of Eggplant and Tomatoes

This salad looks dramatic and tastes wonderful — a perfect way of bringing some of the sunny Mediterranean into your home.

2 large eggplants	⅓ cup dry white wine
a little salt	2 cloves crushed garlic
1 tomato, peeled and sliced evenly	a little chopped marjoram or basil
¼ cup olive oil	

Peel the eggplants and slice fairly thickly. Arrange in a colander, sprinkling salt between layers. Leave to drain for about 30 minutes. Rinse and dry well. Heat some of the olive oil in a large frying pan and fry the eggplant slices until lightly coloured and tender, turning frequently. Keep those that are cooked to one side of the pan while cooking the remainder.

Pour over the wine, letting it bubble. Add the garlic and marjoram or basil and salt and freshly ground pepper to taste. Let it bubble a minute or so then remove from heat. Meanwhile arrange the tomatoes on a large platter and when the eggplants are completely cooled spoon them over.

Serves 6

Use pepper sparingly as it can be an irritant to your digestive system.

Menu 2

Navarin of Lamb with Baby Vegetables

Although our green grocers are regularly getting baby vegetables from the markets they are not essential. The dish with baby vegetables is simply more delicate. In fact some people may miss the flavour of larger turnips that have been exposed to a 'frost'. If using older vegetables take the care to cut them into good even shapes so they still look attractive.

It is essential to take time cutting the lamb, especially in removing the excess fat. Although leaner, more expensive cuts are easier to prepare, they do not have the delicious succulence that a cut such as the shoulder or forequarter will give.

1 forequarter of lamb, boned
1 tablespoon oil
1 teaspoon sugar
3 large tomatoes, peeled, seeded and
  chopped
2 cups good beef stock
2 cloves garlic, bruised and peeled
1 sprig rosemary
1 bouquet garni (bay leaf, sprig of
  thyme and parsley stalks tied
  together)

salt and freshly ground pepper
2 bunches bulbous spring onions
2 bunches tiny white turnips
250g (8oz) slender young green
  beans
30g (1oz) butter

Remove all excess fat from the lamb and cut into large 5cm (2 inch) cubes. Heat the oil in a flameproof casserole and lightly brown the lamb cubes all over, in several lots. Remove each lot as they are browned. When all done return to the pan with the sugar. Stir until browned, about 3 minutes.

Add the prepared tomatoes, stock, garlic, rosemary and bouquet garni and season with salt and pepper. Bring slowly to the boil, reduce heat, half cover and simmer gently for 1½ hours, adding a little more liquid if necessary.

Meanwhile prepare vegetables. Trim the spring onions, and turnips leaving 1cm (½ inch) of their stem still on. Carefully scrape the turnips. Drop the spring onions into boiling salted water, simmer until tender, about 5 minutes. Remove with a slotted spoon and set aside. Drop the turnips into the boiling water and cook for about 10 minutes, until tender. Remove with slotted spoon and set aside. Trim the stem ends of the beans, drop into boiling water and cook about 5 minutes, until just tender, drain and set aside.

Just before serving melt the butter in a sauté pan, add the vegetables and cook over a gentle heat until heated through. Remove the rosemary and bouquet garni from the navarin and spoon on to a serving dish, reserving some of the gravy. Scatter with the vegetables and spoon over the reserved gravy. Serve immediately.

Serves 6

Menu 2

Biscuit Tortoni with Fresh Fruit

In the summer the fresh fruit could be peaches or nectarines, during the cool months, pears. Fresh berries are other alternatives.

$\frac{2}{3}$ cup finely chopped almonds
15g ($\frac{1}{2}$oz) butter
1½ cups crushed amaretti or almond macaroon biscuits
1½ cups fat-reduced cream

1½ tablespoons dark rum or sherry or 2 teaspoons vanilla essence
$\frac{1}{3}$ cup sifted icing sugar
3 ripe scalded peaches, or pears, peeled and sliced

In a heavy frying pan toast the almonds with the butter until golden. Cool, then combine with $\frac{2}{3}$ cup of the crushed biscuits. Set aside 1 tablespoon of this mixture for topping. Stir the rest into ½ cup cream and the rum, sherry or vanilla, then set aside.

Whip the remaining cream until just thickened, sweeten with the icing sugar then continue whipping until thick. Fold in the crumbs, cream and rum mixture and pile into a 15cm (6 inch) round plastic container with a square-edged base. Freeze for about 30 minutes, take out and make a decorative pattern on the top with a spatula. Return to the freezer for at least 3 hours or until firm.

Dip the plastic container into hot water for a few seconds to help turn the tortoni out. Place decorative side up on a plate and smooth the sides if necessary with a hot metal spatula. Press the reserved crushed biscuits into the sides and return to the freezer for one hour more.

Five minutes before serving, remove from the freezer, sprinkle with the reserved topping and arrange the sliced fruit around it.

Serves 6

Amaretti biscuits are Italian almond macaroons, made with egg whites, ground almonds and sugar. They contain no starch.

Menu 3

Tomato Bocconcini Platter

A pretty salad, an Italian inspiration.

6 ripe medium tomatoes   12 basil leaves
3 baby fresh mozzarella cheeses   3 tablespoons virgin olive oil
  (bocconcini)

Wash tomatoes, cut in halves lengthwise. Lay cut slices down on board and make cuts through each almost to base. Cut baby cheeses through into fine slices and tuck a slice of cheese into each, insert a basil leaf into top slice. Arrange cut side down on a large platter, drizzle over the olive oil, strew over the olives. Cover with cling wrap until ready to serve.

Serves 6

Butter and oil are neither starch nor protein, but contain a high fat content so if you have a weight problem watch how much you use of each in your cooking.

Menu 3

Tian of Lamb

This is a special dish, suitable for a dinner party. Ask the butcher to cut the fillet of lamb from a small loin of 6 chops, removing it from the bones and skin. It is an expensive cut but there is no waste and it is very special.

600g (1¼lb) boned lamb loin
1 sprig fresh rosemary
2 garlic cloves
3 tomatoes, peeled, seeded and diced
1 eggplant
250g (8oz) mushrooms
1 shallot
1 onion
olive oil
salt and pepper

SAUCE:
2 cups strong chicken *or* beef stock
fresh rosemary
1 garlic clove
salt and pepper

Trim the lamb fillet of any gristle or fat. Crush the rosemary, rub the lamb with a garlic clove and brush lightly with olive oil. Roll it in the rosemary, season, and reserve.

Clean and slice the mushrooms, slice the eggplant, and season. Peel and chop finely the onion and the shallot.

In a heavy pan heat a spoon of olive oil, add the onion, shallot and cook gently to give colour, for 2 or 3 minutes. Add the mushrooms and cook until they are dry but still moist. Remove and keep warm.

Heat a little oil in a large frying pan. Sauté the slices of eggplant in olive oil and drain on a paper towel.

Cook the lamb in a hot 200°C (400°F) oven for 10 to 15 minutes and let it rest with the door open for 10 more minutes, covered with foil. Cut into fine slices and keep warm.

On a hot plate put first a layer of eggplant overlapping slices to make a circle. Top with mushrooms and arrange on top the slices of lamb as flower petals. Decorate with a small spoon of diced tomatoes on the centre. Pour a spoon of sauce on the top and serve immediately.

SAUCE: Peel a garlic clove and cook it with the chicken stock and a stem of rosemary for 15 minutes. To thicken stock a little, blend a teaspoon of arrowroot soaked with water.

Serves 6

Menu 3

Arugula Salad

1 mignonette lettuce
1 bunch arugula leaves
½ cup finely chopped parsley
 (preferably flat-leaf Italian parsley)

1½ tablespoons red wine vinegar
salt and freshly ground pepper
¼ cup olive oil

Wash lettuce, spin dry and crisp in refrigerator until required. Pick over the arugula leaves and remove and discard any tough stems. Rinse and drain the leaves well and pat dry. Put the leaves in a salad bowl and add the parsley. Put vinegar in a bowl and add salt and pepper to taste. Start beating while gradually adding the oil.

Pour the sauce over the salad and toss lightly.

Serves 6

If you can wean yourself off stimulants such as coffee and tea between meals then do so. Your health is better served by drinking herb teas and alternative coffee preparations.

Tomato and Basil Soup (see A Family Affair)

Mediterranean-Style Stuffed Peppers (see A Family Affair)

Couscous with Vegetables (see An International Menu)

Pineapple and Orange Caramel (see An International Menu)

Pineapple and Orange Caramel

A simple and elegant French dessert using our luscious fresh pineapple and navel oranges.

3-4 navel oranges
½ cup sugar
¼ cup orange-flavoured liqueur or
  kirsch (optional)

1 small ripe pineapple, peeled, cored
  and cut into thick slices (about 6-8)

Cut rind from two of the oranges without removing the white pith. Cut pared rind into thin matchstick strips and drop into boiling water for 5 minutes. Drain. Combine sugar with 3 tablespoons water and bring slowly to the boil so that sugar dissolves. Add peel and boil over high heat until pale caramel, taking care not to burn the peel. Add ½ cup water, stir and leave to cool. Add liqueur, if using.

Arrange pineapple slices on a serving platter. Peel the oranges, removing all traces of white pith and cut across into halves. Arrange orange halves on pineapple slices, scatter the strips of peel over and spoon over the sauce.

Serves 6

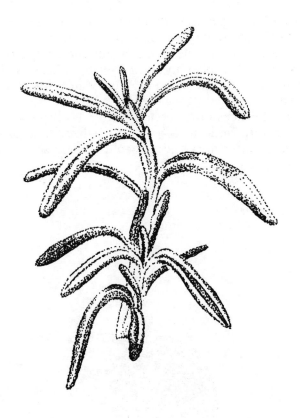

A Taste of Curry

In India many households enjoy vegetarian meals, not only for religious reasons, but they know what they like and what's good for them. Vegetarian or not, a well spiced meal is something we all look forward to with relish.

VEGETARIAN MENU 1 — STARCH
(for 6)
Golden Pilau
Spiced Cauliflower with Eggplant
Spiced Dhal
Curried Zucchini
Sambals and other Accompaniments
Semolini Halva

VEGETARIAN MENU 2 — STARCH
(for 8)
Khichri
Potato and Pea Curry
Eggplant and Potato Curry
Cauliflower and Lentil Curry
Mixed Vegetable Curry
Sambals and other Accompaniments
Semolina Halva

MENU 3 — PROTEIN
(for 8)
Crisp Vegetables with Assorted Dips
Tandoori Chicken in Lettuce Cups
Tikka Kebab
Cucumber and Tomato Sambals
Curried Zucchini
Fresh Pineapple Sherbet
Spears of fresh Pineapple with mint sprigs

Menu 1

Golden Pilau

The whole spices may be removed after cooking, but many consider they add to the interest of the pilau.

2 tablespoons cold pressed
  sunflower oil *or*
30g (1oz) ghee or butter
2 onions, sliced
2-5 sticks cinnamon
2 bay leaves
3 cardamon pods
3 cloves

6 curry leaves, optional
2 teaspoons turmeric or pinch saffron
  threads
2 cups long grain rice
3 cups water
1 cup fresh green peas

Heat the butter or oil in a medium heavy pot. Add onion and cook until soft, then add all the spices and cook 2-3 minutes, tossing several times. Add rice and cook until grains are coated with the oil.

Stir in water, bring to the boil, stir once, cover tightly and cook over a low heat for 18-20 minutes. Meanwhile cook peas and drain. Fork rice lightly, turn into heated bowl, garnish with green peas.

Serves 6

Menu 1

Spiced Cauliflower with Eggplant

1kg (2lb) cauliflower
1 large eggplant
2cm (1 inch) piece peeled fresh
  ginger
½ bunch coriander

1 teaspoon ground chillies½
  teaspoon turmeric
3 tablespoons ghee *or* cold pressed
  sunflower oil

Separate the cauliflower into small florets. Cut unpeeled eggplant into cubes, cover with salted water. Chop the ginger and coriander very finely.

Place a wok or saucepan over moderate heat with the ghee. Add the cauliflower sprigs, ginger and a little salt. Stir-fry then cover and cook over a gentle heat for 5 minutes. Uncover and add chilli and turmeric. Fry for a few minutes and add the drained eggplant. Increase the heat and stir-fry over a moderate heat until the cauliflower is tender, the eggplant cooked and the oil has started lifting to the surface.

Serves 6

          The Food Combining Menu Cookbook

Menu 1

Spiced Dhal

Oriental stores specialising in Indian foods or well-stocked health food stores often keep a variety of lentils. Any type of lentils can be used, though red lentils (masoor dhal) or moong dhal are the quickest cooking types and don't require preliminary soaking as do some of the others.

1 cup red lentils (masoor dhal)
1 onion, sliced
½ teaspoon black peppercorns
4 whole cloves
8 cardamon pods
2 sticks cinnamon

¼ teaspoon salt
½ teaspoon ground chilli
¼ bunch fresh coriander
2 teaspoons ghee *or* cold pressed
  sunflower oil
6 curry leaves

Wash lentils thoroughly and place in a medium saucepan with onion. Add 3 cups of hot water, bring to the boil and simmer covered for 25-30 minutes, or until lentils are half-cooked.

Meanwhile, grind the peppercorns, cloves, 4 cardomons and 1 stick cinnamon. Add to the dhal with salt, chilli and coriander. Simmer for a further 10-15 minutes, until lentils are soft and the consistency of porridge. If there is too much liquid, leave the lid off the pan to speed evaporation. Spoon into a serving bowl.

To serve, heat the ghee with the cinnamon, the remaining cardoman pods, the seeds of which have been crushed, and curry leaves. Pour over the dhal.

Serves 6

The basic rule for food combining is to avoid eating acid fruits such as oranges, pineapples, grapefruit, passionfruit, with starch foods such as cereals, grains, potatoes.

Menu 1

Curried Zucchini

An example of the Indian cook's skill at transforming vegetables into a spicy delight.

500g (1lb) small zucchini
2 tablespoons cold-pressed
 sunflower oil
½ teaspoon cumin seed
1 teaspoon finely chopped fresh
 ginger
1 onion, chopped

1 teaspoon chilli powder
½ teaspoon ground turmeric
1 cup shelled fresh peas
a little salt
2 tablespoons chopped fresh
 coriander

Cut zucchini into thick slices. Heat oil in a frying pan, add cumin seed and fry for a few moments, then add ginger and onion. Fry until golden, add chilli powder and turmeric, stir and add peas and zucchini. Salt lightly, mix well and cover the pan tightly. Cook gently 6-8 minutes or until vegetables are tender. Remove lid and fry until vegetables are dry. Garnish with coriander.

Note: Young chokoes, sliced or cubed, may be substituted for the zucchini.

Serves 6

Menu 1

Sambals and other Accompaniments

Curries are usually served with accompaniments which offer a variety of flavours and textures. Chilled plain yogurt (for protein meals) or fresh sambals are popular. Pappadams (lentil wafers) may be offered at starch based meals only. They are available packaged at delicatessens, health food shops and many supermarkets. Fry one at a time in about 1cm (¼ inch) of hot oil for only a few seconds on each side and drain on paper towels.

Sambals may be red (heating) or white (cooling). Simply add chilli or leave it out according to your preference. Offer one or two of the following, plus a choice of commercial chutneys.

Apple Sambal: Shredded apple plus a little chopped onion and a little salt and chopped green coriander or mint.

Paw Paw or Mango Sambal: Finely diced paw paw or mango with a little salt to taste.

Cucumber Sambal: Finely diced or grated cucumber with a little salt and crushed garlic to taste.

Serves 6

Semolina Halva

This may seem like an overdose of sugar but in fact ½ cup between 8 people is not a lot.

2½ cups water
4 tablespoons vegetable oil
2 cups semolina
½ cup sugar
2-3 tablespoons sultanas

¼ teaspoon finely crushed cardamon seeds (use a pestle and mortar to crush)
½ teaspoon almond essence

Bring the water to the boil in a heavy saucepan. Once it comes to a rolling boil, let the pan sit on a back burner over a low heat.

Heat the oil in a large, preferably non-stick frying pan over a medium heat. Add the semolina, turn the heat to medium low, stir and sauté the semolina for 8-10 minutes or until it turns a warm, golden colour without letting it brown.

Add the sugar to the pan, stirring well. Very slowly begin to pour in the boiling water, stirring all the time. Take a good 2 minutes to do this. When all the water has been added, turn the heat to low. Stir and cook the halva for 5 minutes. Add the sultanas, cardamon and almond essence and cook the halva for a further 5 minutes. Serve warm or at room temperature in individual bowls.

Serves 6

The benefits of food combining are enhanced by avoiding drinking during meals. For maximum benefit try not to drink an hour before and up to an hour after your meal. This way you don't dilute your digestive juices.

Menu 2

Khichri
(Indian Rice and Split Peas)

If the tiny white onions or spring onions are not available use 4 medium brown onions, peeled and quartered with the root ends attached.

½ cup yellow split peas
2 cups long-grain rice, preferably
  Basmati
2 small onions, thinly sliced
2 tablespoons ghee *or* cold-pressed
  safflower oil

12 small white onions
½ teaspoon salt
1 teaspoon each ground cumin and
  garam masala
1 teaspoon grated ginger
1 clove garlic, crushed

Soak the split peas in water to cover overnight. Drain well. Soak the rice in water to cover for 30 minutes. In a large pan sauté half the sliced onion in the oil over a moderately high heat until crisp and golden. Remove with a slotted spoon and set aside. Add the small onions, peeled, and the remaining sliced onion and cook, stirring until they are golden. Add the rice, split peas, salt, cumin, garam masala, ginger and garlic and cook the mixture, stirring for 10 minutes.

Add 4 cups hot water, bring to the boil and simmer the mixture, covered tightly, for 25 minutes. Turn into a heated serving dish and garnish with the reserved sliced onions.

Serves 8

The Food Combining Menu Cookbook

Menu 2

Potato and Pea Curry

45g (1½oz) ghee or 2 tablespoons
  cold-pressed safflower oil
2 medium onions, finely chopped
1 teaspoon cumin seeds
1 teaspoon turmeric
½ teaspoon ground chillies
2 cloves garlic, chopped
½ teaspoon grated ginger

500g (1lb) potatoes, peeled and
  quartered
1 cup green peas
a little salt to taste
1¼ cups warm water
1 teaspoon garam masala
3 tablespoons chopped green
  coriander

Heat the oil in a wok or heavy pan and fry the onion and cumin until golden.
Stir in the turmeric, chillies, garlic and ginger, cook for a few moments then
stir in the potato and peas. Cook for about 5 minutes, stirring frequently.

Add a little salt, pour in the water and bring to the boil. Leave to simmer
over a moderate heat, covered, until potato and peas are tender, about 15
minutes. Sprinkle with the garam masala and coriander and serve.

Serves 8

---

*Most fast foods break food combining rules. Take the pizza;
it's a starch base topped with various ingredients. Only
vegetables are suitable, but don't ruin your good intentions
by adding a protein cheese. What about using hummus
and vegetables on focacci instead?*

Menu 2

Eggplant and Potato Curry

When buying eggplant look for firm, glossy ones with fresh green calyx.

500g (1lb) potatoes
500g (1lb) eggplant
a little salt
2 tablespoons cold-pressed
 sunflower oil
2 teaspoons mustard seeds

1 teaspoon finely chopped fresh
 ginger
1 green chilli, chopped
4 curry leaves (optional)
1 teaspoon turmeric
coriander sprigs to garnish

Boil potatoes and when cool enough to handle, skin them and cut into 2.5cm (1 inch) cubes. Cut unpeeled eggplant into cubes of the same size, place in a bowl and cover with cold, lightly-salted water.

Heat oil in a frying pan on medium heat and add mustard seed. As the seed starts spluttering, add ginger, half the chilli and curry leaves, if using. Fry for a minute, stir in turmeric and add drained eggplant.

Cover and cook for about 5 minutes or until eggplant is tender. Remove lid, turn up heat and add potato. Fry, turning vegetables over once or twice, for 3-4 minutes. Season to taste, adding remaining chilli if liked, and serve strewn with coriander.

Serves 8

Menu 2

Cauliflower and Lentil Curry

1½ cups brown lentils
3 cups water
2 tablespoons ghee *or* cold-pressed
 sunflower oil
2 onions, finely chopped
½ teaspoon chilli powder

1 teaspoon curry powder
½ teaspoon turmeric
1 cup water
a little salt to taste
1 medium cauliflower

Wash lentils and soak for several hours or overnight in cold water. Bring to the boil and simmer until almost tender. Heat oil in a deep saucepan and fry onions until golden. Add spices and cook for a minute or so then add lentils, 1 cup water and a little salt. Bring to the boil. Break cauliflower into small florets and add to the saucepan.

Cover and cook until cauliflower is tender but still firm, about 15-20 minutes, shaking the pan occasionally to prevent sticking.

Serves 8

Menu 2

Mixed Vegetable Curry

The vegetables should be tender but still a little crisp.

2 tablespoons cold-pressed
  sunflower oil
½ teaspoon mustard seeds
6-8 curry leaves
1 teaspoon ground turmeric
2 cloves garlic, crushed
2cm (1 inch) piece green ginger,
  finely grated
pinch chilli powder, optional

3 carrots, cut into strips
250g (8oz) green beans
½ small cabbage, shredded
a little salt to taste

Heat oil and fry mustard seeds and curry leaves for a minute or two. Add turmeric, garlic, ginger and chilli powder and fry until golden. Turn in carrots and beans and fry over medium heat, stirring for 8-10 minutes until vegetables are half cooked and still crisp. Add cabbage and fry for a further 5 to 8 minutes. Add a little salt to taste, cover and simmer for 3 minutes.

Serves 8

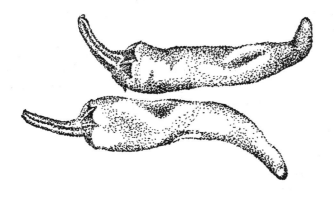

Menu 3

Crisp Vegetables with Assorted Dips

This simple arrangement of crisp, young, fresh, raw or blanched vegetables is offered with walnut chutney or mint and coriander chutney.

Prepare the vegetables as follows:

Carrots: Wash, peel and trim small young carrots, then cut each into quarters or strips. Drop into iced water to crisp.

Cucumber: Use only firm young cucumbers, peel very thinly so as to leave on most of the green, then cut into thick strips.

Spring Onions: Wash, remove outside leaves and trim off root and green tops, about 5cm (2 inches) above the fork of the leaves. Wash well and crisp in refrigerator.

Tomatoes: Use very firm, small tomatoes, preferably the cherry tomato variety. Wash and chill. If using large tomatoes, cut into wedges.

Celery: Wash and cut stalks in 12cm (6 inch) lengths. Drop into a large bowl of iced water and leave to crisp.

Cauliflower: Trim sprigs of cauliflower and wash. Place in iced water.

Asparagus: Break off tough ends. Steam in a pan of lightly salted water about 5 minutes. Drain and refresh under cool water. Drain and place on kitchen towels.

Snow peas or Sugar Snaps: Pinch off the stalk ends and wash thoroughly.

Serves 8

MINT AND CORIANDER CHUTNEY

1 cup coriander leaves
1 cup mint leaves
1 teaspoon sugar
1 tablespoon water

1 tablespoon vinegar or lemon juice
1 green chilli, sliced
½ cup natural, low-fat yogurt

Place all the ingredients except yogurt in a blender and process until fairly smooth. If making by hand, chop the mint, coriander and chilli with the sugar and salt, then gradually add the vinegar and water. Fold the yogurt through. Store in an airtight jar in the refrigerator.

WALNUT CHUTNEY

1 cup shelled walnuts
½ red chilli, chopped
½ cup natural, low-fat yogurt

Put the walnuts and chilli in a blender or food processor with a steel blade. Process using an on-off motion until smooth. Fold the yogurt through and store in an airtight container in the refrigerator.

Menu 3

Tandoori Chicken

India's version of barbecued chicken gets its rich, russet colour from saffron and a few drops of cochineal.

Traditionally tandoori chicken should be cooked in a clay oven called a tandoor, though the recipe can be adapted to suit a conventional oven as done here, or barbecue or griller.

One of the secrets of tandoori chicken is the yogurt marinade — the longer the chicken is left in the marinade, the more authentic will be the finished dish.

1 size 18 chicken, split into halves
1 teaspoon salt
1 tablespoon grated fresh ginger
1½ tablespoons tandoori mix (see below)
1½ cups natural, low-fat yogurt
1 tablespoon lemon juice
45g (1½oz) ghee *or* cold-pressed sunflower oil
extra paprika
onion rings, coriander sprigs, lemon wedges to garnish
crisp lettuce leaves to serve

TANDOORI MIX
2 teaspoons turmeric
1 teaspoon ground paprika
½ teaspoon ground chillies
1 teaspoon garam masala
½ teaspoon ground cardamon
a good pinch saffron threads or powdered saffron

Skin chicken and make slashes into the flesh for the marinade to penetrate. Combine salt, ginger, tandoori mix, yogurt and lemon juice and paprika into a wide glass or china dish. Add chicken and turn to coat thoroughly with the marinade. Cover and chill for at least 6 hours, preferably overnight.

Line a baking dish with a double sheet of aluminium foil and arrange on it the chicken pieces. Drizzle with melted ghee and roast in a hot oven 200°C for 20 minutes. Turn after this time and continue cooking another 15 minutes. Turn again and cook breast side up for the last 10 minutes of cooking. Baste chicken frequently during cooking with the melted ghee and juices from the pan.

Garnish the chicken with onion rings, coriander sprigs and lemon wedges. Offer crisp lettuce leaves to hold the chicken. This dish can be eaten in fingers.

TANDOORI MIX: Mix all ingredients together.

Serves 8

Menu 3

Tikka Kebab

Tikka Kebab are to be found over charcoal barbecues at virtually every street corner in Northern India. They are at their best cooked over a charcoal grill, but they may be grilled under a preheated grill.

750g (1½lb) boned lamb shoulder or leg, cut into 2.5cm (1 inch) cubes
juice of 1 lemon
⅔ cup natural, low-fat yogurt
1 red salad onion *or* 3 small onions, peeled and chopped
2 garlic cloves, peeled and chopped
1 teaspoon turmeric

1 tablespoon vinegar
½ teaspoon ground cumin
¼ teaspoon salt, or to taste
1 teaspoon freshly ground black pepper
1 green or red pepper, cored, seeded and cut into 2.5cm (1 inch) squares
1 lemon, quartered, to garnish

Put the lamb in a bowl and sprinkle with the lemon juice. Put the yogurt, half the onion, the garlic, turmeric, vinegar and seasoning in an electric blender and work until the mixture is evenly blended. Pour over the lamb and stir well. Cover and leave to marinate overnight.

Thread the cubes of meat on kebab skewers, alternating with the green pepper and remaining onion quarters. Barbecue or grill the kebabs, turning frequently, until tender.

Serve hot, garnished with lemon wedges and accompanied by lettuce cups and Tomato and Cucumber Sambals.

Serves 8

Tomato Sambal

Diced or sliced tomato with chopped onion, salt and lemon juice. Sprinkle with chopped chilli, mint or coriander.

Serves 8

Cucumber Sambal

Chilled plain yogurt with finely diced or grated cucumber and salt and crushed garlic to taste.

Serves 8

Fresh Pineapple Sherbet

If you have an electric ice cream machine it's a simple matter to make refreshing sherbets.

1kg (2lb) pineapple
juice of 1 orange
¾ cup sugar

½ cup water
mint leaves to decorate

Peel and core the pineapple and cut into chunks. Purée in a blender or food processor and combine with the orange juice. Chill. Place sugar and water in a saucepan, heat gently until sugar dissolves then boil for 3 minutes. Cool and chill.

Combine fruit and syrup, spoon into container of ice cream machine and process as directed. Transfer to a mould or tray, cover with foil and leave in the freezer for 2 hours. This is best eaten within 6 hours though it will keep for a few days in the freezer. Scoop into small serving bowls and decorate each serving with mint sprigs.

Serves 8

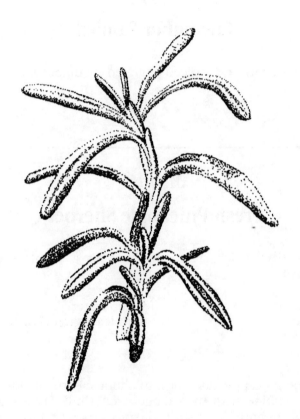

Golden Pilau, Spiced Dhal, Curried Zucchini,
Spiced Cauliflower with Eggplant (see A Taste of Curry)

Fillet of Beef with Wine Fumet (see V.I.P. Dinners)

Golden Nugget Jardinière (see V.I.P. Dinners)

Roman Fried Peppers (see An Italian Affair)

An Italian Affair

Variety is the spice of life, so they say, and anyone seeking a varied diet need look no further than Italy for inspiration.

Food combiners however have a difficulty to overcome when cooking Italian food. Tomatoes which are an acid fruit do not combine well with the starchy pasta, a combination that is well loved in Italy. The following two pasta dishes are excellent examples of how pasta can be served when food combining.

MENU 1— PROTEIN
(for 6)
Roman Fried Peppers
Saltimbocca
Mesclun and Radicchio Salad
Baked Stuffed Peaches

MENU 2 — STARCH
(for 4-6)
Pasta Bows with Fresh Peas
Salad Contadina
Baked Apple Compote

MENU 3
(for 6)
Globe Artichokes
Fusilli with Eggplant and Peppers
Fresh Grapes and Figs on Ice

Menu 1

Roman Fried Peppers

Serve warm or cold.

8 red, yellow, green peppers (capsicums)	2 onions, chopped
	4 ripe tomatoes
3 tablespoons olive or cold-pressed sunflower oil	salt and freshly ground pepper
	a few black olives to decorate

Cut peppers in two, remove ribs and seeds and cut into strips.

Heat the oil in a large frying pan over medium heat, add the onion and pepper strips and cook until the onion begins to colour. Peel and seed tomatoes and roughly chop. Add the tomatoes, season with salt and pepper and cook for 15 minutes. Add some olives and turn the mixture out into a hot serving dish and serve. This dish is also good cold.

Serves 6

Become familiar with herbs. They can be the food combiner's best friend because they are such healthy and neutral flavour boosters.

Menu 1

Saltimbocca

This Roman dish of veal, ham and sage tastes so good that it 'jumps in the mouth', as the Italian name implies. Ask your butcher to cut the veal steaks thinly rather than bat them out which causes them to shrink more during cooking.

4-6 thin veal steaks
4 slices of prosciutto (Italian cured
  ham)
8-12 leaves fresh sage
15g (½oz) butter *or* 2 tablespoons
  light olive oil

salt and freshly ground pepper to
  taste
½ cup dry white wine
fresh parmesan in the piece, shaved
  into curls using a vegetable parer

Cut each steak into 2 or 3 even-sized pieces. Place a thin slice of prosciutto, cut the same size, and a sage leaf on each slice of meat.

Melt butter in a frying pan, add meat slices and brown quickly on both sides, turning carefully so as not to disturb ham and sage leaf. Add a very little salt and freshly ground pepper. Arrange veal on a warm serving dish and keep warm. Add wine to pan and scrape base well. A small nut of butter may be swirled in for a richer sauce. Spoon sauce over veal and top each steak with a piece of shaved parmesan.

Serves 6

Menu 1

Mesclun and Radicchio Salad

Mesclun is a mixture of baby greens such as oak leaf lettuce, tiny cos, butterhead and coral lettuce leaves along with arugula and nasturtium and marigold flower petals. These mixes are appearing in some food shops and are convenient for those in a hurry. Alternatively make your own.

1 tablespoon wine vinegar
3 tablespoons olive oil
1 tablespoon extra virgin olive oil

8 radicchio leaves, rinsed and spun
dry
4-6 cups mesclun

In a large bowl whisk together the vinegar, salt and pepper to taste, add the oils in a stream, whisking until the dressing is emulsified. Toss the radicchio with the dressing and divide it among 4-6 plates, allowing the excess dressing to drip into the bowl. Toss the mesclun with the remaining dressing and divide it among the plates.

Serves 6

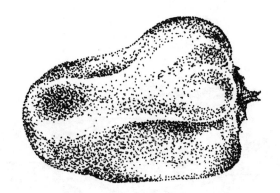

The Food Combining Menu Cookbook

Menu 1

Italian Baked Stuffed Peaches

The base of the filling for these is amaretti biscuits, the Italian almond macaroons.

4-5 large peaches	30g (1oz) butter
2 tablespoons sugar	90g (3oz) crushed amaretti biscuits
1 egg yolk	

Halve the peaches and remove the stones. There is no need to skin them. In a bowl mix together the sugar, egg yolk, butter cut into small pieces and amaretti crumbs. Scoop out a little pulp from each peach half, chop finely and mix with the stuffing mixture. Use this mixture to stuff each peach half.

Arrange the peach halves in a buttered shallow ovenproof dish, pour around a little water, just enough to cover the base. Bake in a moderate oven 180°C (350°F) for about 30 minutes or until tender. Serve hot with cream.

Serves 6

Menu 2

Pasta Bows with Fresh Peas

The peas should be the freshest, sweetest peas you can get. Taste them first because you may have to add a little sugar if they are not sweet enough.

250g (8oz) pasta bows
1 tablespoon olive oil
2 small spring onions, chopped

1 cup shelled fresh peas
salt and freshly ground pepper
2 tablespoons stock or water

To cook pasta, drop into a large pan of boiling, salted water just until tender and drain thoroughly.

Meanwhile heat oil in a saucepan and cook spring onions until soft. Add peas, salt, pepper and stock and cook briskly for 5 minutes. Add a little more stock or water if required and cook gently for another 5 minutes. If the peas were fresh and young they should be cooked enough in this time. Toss the peas with the drained pasta and serve immediately in 4 bowls.

Serves 4-6

Pasta poses a problem because we normally mix it with either tomato or meat sauce and cheese. Clever food combiners can skirt round this by using plenty of fresh vegetables and herbs.

The Food Combining Menu Cookbook

Menu 2

Salad Contadina

One lovely, big hearty salad, perfect for family meals, picnics, or outdoor meals.

500g (1lb) new potatoes, boiled and sliced
500g (1lb) string beans, cooked in lightly salted boiling water
1 can cannellini beans
1 quantity Pepper Salad (see below)
½ cup Vinaigrette (see below)
1 purple salad onion, sliced and broken into rings
2 tablespoons chopped basil

VINAIGRETTE DRESSING:
½ cup light olive oil *or* cold-pressed sunflower oil
2 tablespoons wine vinegar
1 teaspoon Dijon mustard
1 crushed clove garlic
salt and freshly ground black pepper

PEPPER SALAD:
3 peppers, red or green
2 tablespoons olive oil
a little wine or cider vinegar *or* a squeeze of lemon juice
1 clove garlic, chopped
fresh herbs (parsley, oregano, chives, basil)

Toss the potatoes, beans, and cooked dried beans with the vinaigrette and in a salad platter, surround with a decorative ring of the Pepper Salad and onions, and scatter with the basil.

VINAIGRETTE DRESSING: Combine oil, vinegar, mustard, garlic, salt and freshly ground black pepper in a screw-top jar. Shake well just before using.

PEPPER SALAD: Cut peppers into quarters, remove seeds, etc. Lay out on a grilling tray and roast under a red hot grill until blistered. Place in dish and dress with olive oil, lemon juice, garlic and herbs, tossing lightly. Allow to come to room temperature.

Serves 4-6

Menu 2

Baked Apple Compote

A spicy apple compote, beautiful for a winter dessert. Any left over makes a delicious breakfast fruit.

6 to 8 apples
3 tablespoons fresh lemon juice
2 tablespoons mild-flavoured honey
  (such as rainforest acacia)
¼ cup unsweetened apple juice
1 stick cinnamon
½ teaspoon ground allspice

¼ to ½ teaspoon freshly grated
  nutmeg
½ teaspoon vanilla essence
2 tablespoons currants
½ cup natural, low-fat yogurt for
  topping

Preheat the oven to moderate 180° (350°F). Lightly butter a 8-10 cup baking dish. Peel, core and slice the apples. Toss with the lemon juice in the prepared baking dish. Add the remaining ingredients except yogurt and toss together. Bake in the preheated oven for 45 minutes to 1 hour. Serve warm or at room temperature, topped with plain, low fat yogurt. The fruit will keep several days in the refrigerator.

Note: If liked this may be cooked in a heavy saucepan or casserole on top of the stove. Add an extra half a cup of apple juice and cook very gently, covered, until apples are tender.

Serves 4-6

Cut down on your fat intake by substituting natural skim-milk yogurt or cashew nut cream for cream or ice-cream. You'll enjoy the change I'm sure.

Globe Artichokes

At the beginning of the season elongated artichokes are available. They have hardly any choke and even if they do have, it is usually not worth worrying about.

4-6 globe artichokes
2 tablespoons olive oil
1 onion, sliced
a sprig of oregano
2 large cloves garlic

½ cup white wine *or* water
1 tablespoon freshly chopped parsley
a little salt and freshly ground
  pepper

Remove the tough outer leaves of the artichokes and cut one-quarter off the top of each, trimming the stalks. Cut lengthwise into quarters and put into cold water to cover. Drain and dry thoroughly.

In a heavy saucepan combine onion, oregano, garlic, bay leaf, white wine and parsley with salt and pepper. Add artichokes, cover and simmer slowly for 40 minutes. Artichokes are cooked when a leaf pulls out easily. Serve warm.

To eat, pull out a leaf at a time, scraping away the tender base of each leaf by pulling through your teeth. Remove any hairy choke with a spoon and eat the artichoke heart.

Serves 6

Menu 3

Fusilli with Eggplant and Peppers

2 medium eggplants
½ cup cold pressed sunflower *or*
  olive oil
1 clove garlic
2 each red and green peppers
a little salt

1-2 tablespoons chopped basil
¼ cup slivered black olives
½ cup chopped parsley
freshly ground pepper
about 300g (10oz) dried fusilli

Peel the eggplant and cut into small dice. Pour half the olive oil into a frying pan and add the garlic and the diced eggplant. Fry gently until tender. Meanwhile halve and seed the peppers and cut into thin strips.

Pour the remaining oil into the frying pan and add the pepper strips. Cook for about 5 minutes and add salt, pepper and basil.

Meanwhile, cook the fusilli in boiling, salted water for 10-12 minutes until 'al dente'. Drain. Toss in the eggplant, peppers and olives and sprinkle with parsley, mixing well.

Serves 6

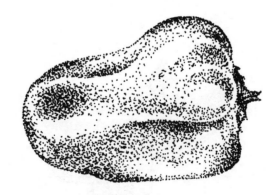

The Food Combining Menu Cookbook

V.I.P. Dinners

These menus are designed to honour a very special person, along with a few selected friends. The dishes are elegant and demand a certain amount of care in the preparation and presentation.

MENU 1 — PROTEIN
(for 6)
Cream of Asparagus Soup
Fillet of Beef with Wine Fumet
or Pan-Grilled Salmon
or Ocean Trout with Sage
Steamed Baby Green Beans
Mesclun and Radicchio Salad (see page 84)
Gratin of Strawberries with Sabayon Sauce

MENU 2— STARCH
(for 6)
Mushroom Consomme
Golden Nuggets Jardiniere
French Apple Tart

Menu 1

Cream of Asparagus Soup

The soup is enriched with a little cream at the end.

1kg (2lb) asparagus
6 cups chicken stock
1 small onion, chopped
30g (1oz) butter

¼ cup cream
1 egg yolk
a little salt and freshly ground
 pepper

Cut away the tougher sections of the asparagus stalks. Cut off the tips and reserve. Peel the rest and cut into short pieces. Put the chicken stock on to boil and add the asparagus chunks. Cook for about 10 minutes then add the tips. Cook for a further 5 minutes or until tender. Remove the tips and set aside. Remove the chunks with a slotted spoon to a blender, reserving the liquid. Purée the drained chunks in a blender.

In the pan cook the chopped onion in the butter until softened, about 5 minutes. Add the reserved cooking liquid and simmer gently for 5 minutes. Gradually add the asparagus purée. Blend the cream with the egg yolk in a small bowl and stir in some of the hot asparagus liquid. Stir this mixture back into the pan and heat gently without allowing to boil. Season to taste with a little salt and pepper and serve with the asparagus tips added to the individual servings.

Serves 6

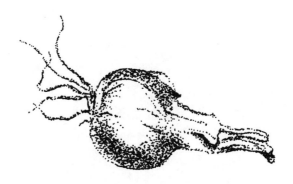

The Food Combining Menu Cookbook

Menu 1

Fillet of Beef with Wine Fumet

One of the simplest dishes in the world to do well. The wine sauce is made from the pan juice. Serve warm with young green beans.

1.5kg (3lb) beef fillet
30g (1oz) butter
2 tablespoons brandy

WINE FUMET:
1 cup red wine
2 tablespoons butter
a little salt and freshly ground black
    pepper

Remove all tissue and skin from fillet with a sharp knife. If necessary, after trimming, tie fillet into a neat shape with string.

Heat butter in a flameproof baking dish and brown fillet on all sides over moderate heat. Warm brandy in a small saucepan, set alight and pour over beef. Shake pan until the flames subside, spooning juices over meat.

Place baking dish in a preheated hot oven 200°C (400°F) and roast for 15 minutes for very rare beef, 20 minutes for medium-rare. Leave fillet in turned-off oven for 15 minutes. Remove to a serving platter and make sauce.

WINE FUMET: Add wine to the baking dish and place over moderate heat, scraping up any crusty pieces. Add butter and seasoning and stir until piping hot and reduced slightly. Cut beef into thick slices and pour the sauce over or serve separately at the table. Serve with steamed baby green beans and garnish with watercress, if liked.

Serves 6

Fats such as unsalted butter and cold pressed oil combine with either starch or protein food, but they should be used sparingly, for your health's sake.

Menu 1

Pan-Grilled Salmon or Ocean Trout with Sage

Use a preheated grill, brushing the racks well with oil. Alternatively use a ribbed grill pan (sometimes called a grillet).

oil for brushing the pan and the
  salmon
4 thick Atlantic salmon *or* ocean trout
  steaks (fillets can be used but will
  take less time to cook and more
  room in the pan)

a little sea salt to taste
1 tablespoon freshly chopped sage
  leaves
2 tablespoons extra virgin olive oil

Rinse the salmon steaks very lightly and pat dry with paper kitchen towels. Heat a grill or ribbed grill pan over a moderately high heat until hot then brush the rack or pan with vegetable oil. When the oil is hot but not smoking add the fish steaks which have been brushed with oil and sprinkled with sage leaves. Cook for about 6 minutes, turning once.

To serve, peel away the skin of the steaks and arrange on heated plates. Sprinkle immediately with the sea salt and drizzle with the olive oil.

Serves 6

If you want to serve cocktail food that suits food combiners then put away the crackers and offer dips and cheeses together with raw vegetables such as carrots, zucchini, apple, and celery.

Gratin of Strawberries with Sabayon Sauce

Even less flavoursome strawberries that are out of peak season can taste good this way.

2 punnets strawberries
3 egg yolks
3 tablespoons caster sugar
1 tablespoon cold water

2 tablespoons thick cream
1 tablespoon eau-de-vie de fraise
 (strawberry liqueur) or kirsch
icing sugar

Arrange the berries on 6 individual heatproof gratin dishes. Whisk the egg yolks and sugar together in a bowl over a pan of simmering water, until thickened. Whisk in the cream and liqueur.

Spoon the sauce over the strawberries, sprinkle lightly with icing sugar and place under a preheated very hot grill for a few moments until lightly coloured.

Serves 6

Menu 2

Mushroom Consomme

This soup seems unusual but is superb.

1kg (2lb) mushrooms
1kg (2lb) onions, peeled and
  chopped
a little salt
a squeeze lemon juice
1 tablespoon madeira *or* dry sherry
  (optional)

GARNISH:
thin julienne strips of spring onion,
  very thinly sliced button
  mushrooms and a few sprigs of
  watercress.

In a large pan add the mushrooms and onions to 8 cups water, salt and lemon juice. Bring slowly to the boil, reduce heat, cover and simmer gently for 1½ hours. Strain through a fine colander and return to the pan.

Add madeira, if using, and a little salt and pepper to taste and reheat gently. Ladle the soup into heated bowls and sprinkle with the garnishes.

Serves 6

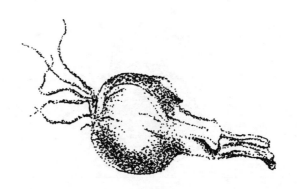

Pasta Bows with Peas (see An Italian Affair)

Barbecued Red Peppers, Charcoal Roasted Corn on the Cob,
Butternut Pumpkin in the Embers, Fried Eggplant (see It's a Barbecue)

Eggplant Lasagne (see Meals for Vegetarian Friends)

Strawberry Pignola with Fresh Ricotta
(see Meals for Vegetarian Friends)

Menu 2

Golden Nuggets Jardinière

Small golden nugget pumpkins filled with perfect young vegetables. I like to cook one or two extra pumpkins in case some have started to deteriorate, something you will only know after they've been cooked and opened.

6-8 golden nugget pumpkins
a selection of perfect vegetables such
  as broccoli, asparagus, baby button
  squash, both the yellow and green,
  button mushrooms, spring onions,
  and for the colour, red pepper

60g (2oz) butter
a few sprigs of thyme or rosemary
salt and freshly ground pepper
4 tablespoons freshly chopped
  parsley

Wash the pumpkins, dry them and rub with a little oil. Place on a baking dish and bake in a preheated, moderately hot oven 190°C (375°F) for 40-50 minutes, until tender when pierced with a skewer.

Meanwhile prepare vegetables. Break the broccoli into small florets. Drop into a little boiling salted water and blanch for 3 minutes. Trim the spring onions and blanch for 3 minutes. Cut the asparagus into short lengths and blanch for 2 minutes. Cut the baby squash into small pieces, the peppers into strips and trim the mushrooms. Heat the butter into a sauté pan, add the squash and spring onions, then the asparagus, then the pepper, and finally the broccoli, each at 1 minute intervals. Continue to sauté over a high heat for 1 more minute. Season with salt and pepper and stir in half the parsley.

Cut a cap off each pumpkin, scoop out the seeds with a spoon and discard. Fill each with the vegetable mixture and set the cap on the side. Scatter with remaining parsley and serve immediately.

Serves 6

Menu 2

French Apple Tart

Golden Delicious apples are the best to use for a tart such as this. They get a nice caramel tinge around the edges, providing very much the look of a beautiful French apple tart. Serve warm or cold.

750g (1½lb) dessert apples
15g (½oz) butter
1 tablespoon caster sugar

GLAZE:
¼ cup apricot jam
1 tablespoon water
squeeze lemon juice

PÂTE SUCRÉE
(Sweet Flan Pastry)
1 cup plain flour
pinch of salt
60g (2oz) unsalted butter
2 tablespoons caster sugar
1 egg yolk
1 tablespoon water
2 drops vanilla essence

Dust pastry board and roll the Pâte Sucrée to fit a 20cm (8 inch) flan ring. Press the dough well into the sides without stretching the pastry and trim the excess. Prick the base with a fork and chill for a further 15 minutes.

To fill the tart, peel, quarter and slice the apples into the pastry, continually levelling them. Arrange the last layer of apples, overlapping in circles. Dust with the sugar and brush with the melted butter. Bake in a preheated moderately hot oven 190°C (375°F) for 30-35 minutes.

After 20 minutes gently lift off the flan ring to finish cooking. Remove from the oven and brush the apples with the glaze. To make the glaze, heat all ingredients together until clear and smooth. Rub through a sieve into a bowl and use immediately while still warm.

PÂTE SUCRÉE *(Sweet Flan Pastry):* Sift the flour with the salt on to the pastry board or marble slab and make a well in the centre. Place the remaining ingredients into the centre. Work the centre ingredients together with the fingertips of one hand. The movement of the fingertips working on these centre ingredients is rather like that of a chicken pecking corn. Add water.

Using a metal spatula, quickly draw in the flour. Knead the pastry lightly until smooth. Wrap in greaseproof paper and chill for 1 hour or more before using. Bake in a moderately hot oven 190°C (375°F) until the pastry is a pale biscuit colour.

This is sufficient for a 20cm (8 inch) flan case or 1 dozen tartlets. It is best chilled before baking, and again after it has been rolled out. Prick the base just before placing in the oven.

Serves 6

It's a Barbecue

Casual, relaxed, enjoying the open air; it's just what we all need to make us feel good. Here is a new look at barbecues with exotic flavours and spices. Invite a few friends to enjoy them with you.

MENU 1 — PROTEIN
(for 8)
Crisp Vegetables with Assorted Dips (see page 76)
Thai Barbecue Chicken
Kofta Kebabs *or* Barbecued Red Mullet
Thai Cucumber Salad
Green Salad
Tropical Fruit in Ginger Wine

MENU 2 — STARCH
(for 8)
Poor Man's Caviar
Charcoal Roasted Corn on the Cob
Butternut Pumpkin in the Embers
Barbecued Red Peppers and Eggplant
Foil-Wrapped Potatoes
Fruit Kebabs

Menu 1

Thai Barbecued Chicken

Chicken pieces are marinated with a spice paste and cooked over glowing coals or under a griller.

2kg (4lb) chicken pieces
1 bunch coriander
2 cloves garlic, peeled
3 small red chillies, halved and
  seeded
1 teaspoon each turmeric and curry
  powder

1 teaspoon sugar
a little salt
3 tablespoons Thai fish sauce
1 punnet snow pea shoots
1 crisp lettuce

Remove all excess fat from the chicken pieces and pat dry with kitchen towels. Wash the coriander thoroughly, including the roots, and cut the roots off at the stems. Reserve the green tops for garnishing. Place the roots in a blender or food processor with the peeled garlic and chillies, the spices and sugar and process to a coarse paste. Add the fish sauce and continue to grind until smooth. Place the chicken pieces in a large shallow ceramic dish and rub all over with the spice paste, preferably using thin rubber gloves. Leave to marinate for several hours if possible.

Arrange the chicken pieces on a grill and grill or barbecue until well browned and tender, turning once and basting once or twice more. Arrange on a serving platter lined with snow pea shoots, garnish with coriander and accompany with cucumber salad. Serve with a large bowl of crisp lettuce leaf cups.

Serves 8

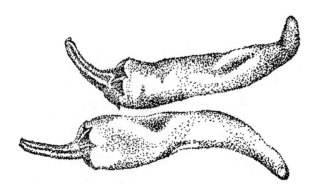

The Food Combining Menu Cookbook

Menu 1

Kofta Kebabs

Good minced meat is liberally spiced, beaten well, moulded on skewers then barbecued or grilled.

500g (1lb) best minced steak	freshly ground pepper
1 small onion, finely chopped	1 teaspoon lemon juice
2 tablespoons natural, low-fat yogurt	½ teaspoon grated lemon rind
a little salt to taste	natural, low-fat yogurt to serve
½ teaspoon each ground ginger, coriander, cumin, allspice, nutmeg	

Mix all ingredients, beating thoroughly so the meat absorbs the yogurt. Divide into 6 portions and shape each around a thick skewer, in a long cigar shape.

Heat grill, place kebabs on a sheet of aluminium foil and place under grill. Cook for 6-10 minutes, turning regularly until brown all over. Offer a bowl of natural yogurt to spoon over kebabs.

Serves 8

Menu 1

Barbecued Red Mullet (or Sardines)

These delicious little fish, called 'rougets' in France where they are much prized, mustn't be confused with the similar in appearance yet inferior, gurnard. Red mullet are usually about 10cm (4 inches) long and prepared by slitting the stomach to remove the entrails except for the liver which is considered a delicacy by some. Rinse in lightly salted water, dry carefully (as the flesh is delicate) with kitchen paper towels. Fresh sardines can be used in place of the red mullet.

24 fresh tiny red mullet, or several larger ones, cleaned	a little salt and freshly ground pepper
¼ cup oil	3 lemons, quartered
fresh vine leaves	chopped parsley

Place the prepared fish in a bowl, season them lightly with salt and pepper, brush liberally with oil, inside and out. Wrap in vine leaves and arrange on rack over glowing coals or under a hot grill and cook for 2-3 minutes on each side, 5 minutes each side for larger fish. Arrange on a hot serving platter and garnish with the lemon quarters and a generous sprinkling of parsley.

Serves 8

It's a Barbecue

Menu 1

Thai Cucumber Salad

2 dried red chillies, seeded and
  soaked in water for 5 minutes
1 clove garlic
2 tablespoons Thai fish sauce
½ teaspoon sugar
2 tablespoons cold-pressed
  sunflower oil

juice of ½ lemon or lime
4 small cucumbers
2cm (1 inch) young green ginger
1 tablespoon chopped coriander
  leaves

Pound or blend the dried chillies and garlic to a paste. Mix in the fish sauce, sugar, oil and lemon or lime juice. Peel the cucumber thinly and cut into cubes or strips. Peel the ginger and cut into very fine slivers. In a bowl, toss the cucumber and ginger with the sauce mixture and sprinkle with the coriander leaves.

Serves 8

Menu 1

Green Salad

A selection of lettuce leaves (or
  mixed salad greens)
2 tablespoons wine vinegar
1 clove garlic, finely chopped

6 tablespoons light olive oil or cold-
  pressed sunflower oil
a little salt and freshly ground
  pepper

Rinse the lettuce leaves and shake (or whirl in basket) off any excess moisture. Blend the vinegar and garlic in a mixing bowl. Stir with a whisk, gradually adding the oil. Add salt and pepper to taste. Toss the lettuce with the dressing at the very last moment.

Serves 8

Tropical Fruit in Ginger Wine

The preparation of delectable fruit plates takes time but is so light, luscious and refreshing it is worth it. The ginger wine gives a lovely taste. The flaming removes the alcohol.

1 small ripe pineapple
2 oranges
1 ripe mango
6 tablespoons ginger wine
flaked almonds, toasted

Peel, core and slice the pineapple. Peel orange, removing all the pith, and slice. Peel and slice the mango. The fruit should all be sliced on a large plate to catch the juice.

Arrange the sliced fruit on individual plates. In a ladle flame the ginger wine and pour over the fruit, adding the juice from the fruit. Scatter with toasted flaked almonds.

Serves 8

The ideal meal plan in a day is to have one fruit meal (which is best kept to breakfast), one protein meal and one starch meal. These two can be interchanged as lunch and dinner, according to your day.

Poor Man's Caviar

This dish can be made just before the rest of the food is put on the barbecue. The charcoal grilling gives a smoky flavour that is delicious and it doesn't take long to make with a food processor at hand. Alternatively the eggplant may be cooked in a moderate oven.

2 medium eggplants, weighing about 500g (1lb)	1 onion, grated
	2 tablespoons chopped parsley
3 cloves garlic, crushed	2 tablespoons olive oil
a little salt	squeeze lemon juice

Remove the stem from the eggplants and grill whole directly over the barbecue. Turn them over until their skins are blistered and quite soft, about 15-20 minutes. Peel and finely chop the flesh while still hot (use a food processor if you wish). Add the garlic, salt and onion and beat well. Add the parsley and slowly beat in the olive oil and lemon juice. The mixture should be the consistency of mayonnaise. Put in a serving bowl and surround with crisp vegetable sticks and crackers or pitta bread.

Serves 8

Menu 2

Charcoal Roasted Corn on the Cob

There are several ways of cooking corn on the cob over a barbecue.

Use unhusked ears of young plump corn. Pull down the husk to remove silk and any damaged corn kernels. Replace the husk and run into it as much water as it will hold. Close the husk by twisting it and put the ears on a rack over glowing coals for 20-25 minutes, turning frequently. Before serving remove the husks using tongs or gloves.

Alternatively the husk and silk can be removed and the corn cob wrapped in heavy duty foil. Wrap securely and place in barbecue coals for 15 minutes, turning several times.

Serves 8

Menu 2

Butternut Pumpkin in the Embers

Butternut pumpkins are excellent cooked at a barbecue, either on the grill or in the embers. Either way, several layers of heavy duty foil are needed.

1 butternut pumpkin
a little butter
freshly ground parsley
a little salt and freshly ground
  pepper

Wash the butternut pumpkin, halve lengthwise and scoop out and discard the seeds. Replace the halves together with a little butter in the centre if liked and wrap up tightly in several layers of heavy duty foil. Bury in the embers of the barbecue and cook, turning a few times for 20-25 minutes. Unwrap carefully using tongs or gloves and place on a serving platter, sprinkle with parsley and season with salt and freshly ground pepper.

Note: If cooking the butternut pumpkin on the grill of the barbecue separate the two halves, wrap in foil and cook, turning several times, for 20-25 minutes.

Serves 8

Menu 2

Barbecued Red Peppers and Eggplant

This dish makes lighting the barbecue very worthwhile.

6 large red peppers
1 eggplant, sliced thickly
½ cup olive oil

2 cloves garlic, finely chopped
coarse salt and freshly ground
  pepper

Quarter the peppers and flick out the seeds. Prepare the eggplant. Combine the remaining ingredients in a large bowl. Arrange the pepper quarters and eggplant slices on the barbecue rack over glowing coals and cook, turning once until soft and lightly charred. Transfer immediately to the oil, garlic, salt and pepper mixed in a bowl and toss before serving.

Serves 8

Menu 2

Foil-Wrapped Potatoes

Choose even-sized medium baking potatoes, scrub them well and cook in salted water for 15 minutes. Drain, wipe with a tea towel, rub with a little butter and wrap each potato in foil. Cook on the coals or on the barbecue grill for 20 minutes. Test with a skewer. To serve, pull back the foil, cut a cross on the top and squeeze to open. If liked add a tiny dab of butter with freshly ground pepper and salt.

Serves 8

Menu 2

Fruit Kebabs

Rather than going against the rule of combining acid with starch, cut the bananas just at the last moment rather than sprinkling with lemon juice to avoid discoloration.

3 kiwifruit, peeled and quartered
3 bananas, quartered
2 pears, peaches or nectarines, cut
  into thick wedges

MARINADE:
2 tablespoons honey, warmed
1 teaspoon grated orange rind
2 tablespoons melted butter
1 tablespoon rum (optional)
¼ teaspoon ground cinnamon

First mix marinade ingredients in a large bowl. Put prepared fruit in bowl, turn to coat evenly with marinade then thread fruit on to skewers. Barbecue, turning and brushing frequently with marinade until fruit is golden and hot.

Serves 8

The Food Combining Menu Cookbook

Meals for Vegetarian Friends

It's a sign of the times. We seem to be gathering more friends every day who are vegetarian. When it comes to entertaining them there should be no big problems, after all much of the best food in the world is vegetarian. Each of these menus serves four to six, depending on appetites.

MENU 1 — PROTEIN
(for 4-6)
Mesclun and Radicchio Salad (see page 84)
Eggplant Lasagne (without Pasta)
Baked Caramel Pears

MENU 2 — STARCH
(for 4-6)
Spaghetti Squash with Fresh Peas
Potato Gnocchi
Mesclun and Radicchio Salad (see page 84)
French Apple Tart (see page 98)

MENU 3 — STARCH
(for 4-6)
Golden Squash Salad with Cumin
Bucatini with Broccoli
Baked Caramel Pears (see page 109)

MENU 4 — PROTEIN
(for 4-6)
Eggplant Charlotte *or*
Zucchini and Pepper Frittata
Mesclun and Radicchio Salad (see page 84)
Strawberry Pignola with Fresh Ricotta

Menu 1

Eggplant Lasagne
(without pasta)

It is quite usual in Italy for vegetable dishes such as this to be eaten as a meal course, especially in Naples, where the local vegetables (especially the tomatoes and eggplants) are so flavoursome.

2 eggplants
a little salt
olive oil *or* cold-pressed sunflower
   oil
1kg (2lb) ripe tomatoes, peeled and
   chopped

3 sprigs basil
salt and freshly ground pepper
1 cup parmesan cheese, grated
250g (8oz) mozzarella cheese, sliced
1 egg, beaten

Cut eggplant lengthwise into thin slices. Sprinkle with salt and leave to drain for 30 minutes on a plate set at an angle, or in a colander to rid the vegetable of its bitter juices. Rinse and dry thoroughly. Fry in olive oil or vegetable oil until golden brown on both sides. Drain on paper towels. Add the tomatoes and basil to the same pan and cook over a brisk heat until the tomatoes are soft and thick, resembling a sauce. Season with a little salt and pepper.

Lightly grease a shallow ovenproof dish and arrange a layer of eggplant slices in it. Sprinkle with parmesan cheese, cover with a few slices of mozzarella cheese, spread with some tomato and the beaten egg.

Continue to layer remaining ingredients in this manner, ending with a top layer of eggplant. Lightly sprinkle the casserole with remaining parmesan cheese and bake in a moderate oven 190°C (375°F) for about 40 minutes.

May be served hot or at room temperature.

Serves 4-6

Menu 1

Baked Caramel Pears

A simple dish of pears baked with sugar and finished in the oven with a vanilla and kirsch-flavoured cream. The pears should be perfectly ripe though still firm.

60g (2oz) butter
6 tablespoons sugar
4-6 ripe pears, peeled, halved and
  cored

½ cup cream
1 teaspoon vanilla
2 tablespoons kirsch or brandy

Melt half the butter in a shallow ovenproof serving dish, just large enough to take the pear halves in one layer. Sprinkle the dish with half the sugar. Cut the pears across into thick slices, not quite through, and arrange cut side down in the dish. Sprinkle with remaining sugar and top each pear with a piece of butter. Bake uncovered in a preheated very hot oven 225°C (425°F) for 20 minutes, basting several times with cooking juices.

   Combine cream, vanilla and kirsch. Pour over pears and bake 20 minutes longer or until cream mixture is slightly thickened. Serve warm.

Serves 4-6

Menu 2

Spaghetti Squash with Fresh Peas

Vegetable spaghetti looks like a long melon, with a smooth skin like a marrow and is similar in colour to a rockmelon. This fascinating and delicious vegetable has a surprising centre after being boiled and split — a mass of thready flesh, like a tangle of pasta.

1 spaghetti squash	2 cups fresh peas, cooked until
salt	tender and drained
butter	freshly ground pepper

Push a skewer into the spaghetti squash to make a hole. This helps the centre to cook more quickly. Boil in a large pan of salted water for 40-50 minutes, depending on the size. Test with a skewer to see if the inside is tender. Drain and cool for a few minutes then split in half to reveal the strings of flesh inside. The seeds are removed at this stage. Turn the strings of flesh out into a serving bowl, using a large fork to help pull them away from the sides.

Melt some butter and add to the spaghetti squash together with the peas. Season well with freshly ground pepper and toss using two forks.

Serves 4-6

Remember nuts are an excellent source of protein, particularly hazelnuts, almonds, and walnuts, so use them to add flavour when cooking protein meals. If you are a vegetarian they are a must in your diet each day.

Menu 2

Potato Gnocchi
(Gnocchi di Patate)

1kg (2lb) old floury potatoes
1¾ cups plain flour
salt

60g (2oz) unsalted butter
1-2 tablespoons roughly chopped
    sage leaves

Boil the potatoes and place in a pan with just enough water to cover. Cover and boil the potatoes until tender without letting them break up. Drain and peel them as soon as you can handle them. Mash and rub through a metal sieve using the base of a glass jar to help.

As soon as the purée is cool enough to handle start beating in the flour, then, as the dough stiffens, turn it out to knead on a floured board. Knead until you obtain a soft, but elastic, dough.

Next, take a handful of the dough, knead lightly, using flour to dust your hands and the work surface, and roll into a sausage shape. Cut into 2cm (1in) slices.

Now take a large, slim-pronged fork with round edges. A wooden fork is best, but difficult to find. Hold it in your left hand with the prongs down. Take a slice of dough and, with your thumb, squeeze the dough against the prongs, letting the gnocchi roll off on to a clean cloth. Repeat with remaining dough. The gnocchi should curl up into crescent-shaped ribbed shells as they roll off the fork.

A simpler alternative, if you are finding this shaping difficult to master, is to press each slice of dough gently around your finger to curve it, using a fork to make the ribbed grooves. The shaping is not just decorative. It serves to thin out the centre of the gnocchi so that they cook evenly and the grooves serve to trap the flavours of the sauce.

Drop the gnocchi (about 20 at a time) into a large pan of boiling salted water. When they are ready they will float to the surface. Cook them just another 10 seconds then remove with a slotted spoon to a warm dish.

Brown butter with the chopped sage in a small pan and pour over gnocchi. Toss lightly and serve immediately.

Serves 4-6

Menu 3

Golden Squash Salad with Cumin

We recognise that yellow, green and red vegetables are all good for us. Here is a delicious dish of these vegetables combined.

250g (8oz) butternut pumpkin
8 tiny patty pan squash, halved across
  or 6 tiny zucchini, cut into chunks
1 small red pepper, cut into strips
1 teaspoon cumin seeds

1 tablespoon shredded mint
½ red onion, finely sliced
½ teaspoon sugar
2 tablespoons extra light olive oil

Peel the pumpkin, halve and seed and cut across into slices. Place with squash or zucchini in a steamer over boiling water and steam until just tender. Place with pepper strips in a bowl to cool.

In a small frying pan lightly toast the cumin seeds until they are fragrant without burning. Transfer to a plate and when cool crush between 2 sheets of wax paper or use a mortar and pestle. Combine half the toasted cumin, mint, onion, sugar and mix well. Spoon over the vegetables and toss gently together with the olive oil. Dust with the remaining toasted cumin.

Serves 4-6

It makes good sense to cut down on oil when cooking. Save it as a flavouring and use good quality, non-stick cookware when frying.

Menu 3

Bucatini with Broccoli

In Southern Italy this is a popular way with pasta. Sometimes tiny zucchini or cauliflower are used instead of the broccoli. All are equally good.

1 large head of broccoli
salt
6 spring onions, finely chopped
3 tablespoons olive oil
2 tablespoons currants

1 cup dry white wine
pepper
¼ teaspoon saffron (optional)
375g-500g (12oz-1lb) bucatini

Trim and wash the broccoli, cut into small pieces, discarding any tough stem, then boil in salted water until tender. Drain, reserving ½ cup of the water.

Fry the onion in 2 tablespoons olive oil until soft, then add the currants. Cook a minute or so and pour in the wine and continue to cook, uncovered, for 5 minutes or until reduced. Add the broccoli, a little salt to taste, pepper and saffron, if using, and the reserved water. Cook for 10 minutes, gently crushing the broccoli into the sauce with a wooden spoon. Meanwhile cook the bucatini in plenty of boiling water until *al dente*. Drain and mix with the sauce. Serve hot.

Serves 4-6

Eggplant Charlotte

2kg (4lb) eggplant
½ cup olive oil *or* cold-pressed
  sunflower oil
½ cup water
2 sprigs fresh oregano or thyme
1 large clove garlic, finely chopped
salt and freshly ground pepper
5 eggs
⅓ cup freshly grated parmesan

TOMATO SAUCE
1kg (2lb) ripe red tomatoes
6 tablespoons olive oil
10 basil leaves or fresh sprigs
salt and freshly ground pepper

Wash the eggplant and wipe dry. Cut enough into slices to line the base and sides of a 20cm (8 inch) fairly deep cake tin. Heat half the oil and fry these slices lightly on each side. Line the cake tin with these browned slices.

Cut the remaining eggplant into cubes and add to pan with garlic. Sauté lightly in the remaining oil for a few minutes then add the water and oregano and garlic. Season with a little salt and pepper, cover and cook gently, stirring frequently to prevent catching until eggplant is soft and tender. Add more water if necessary. Purée the eggplant coarsely in a food processor then allow to cool.

In a bowl beat the eggs lightly with a fork, adding the cheese and cooled eggplant mixture. Check for seasoning, adding more salt and pepper if necessary. Turn the mixture into the prepared cake tin and smooth the surface. Bake in a preheated hot oven 200°C (400°F) for 45-50 minutes or until set. The centre will cook the last so should be checked by inserting a knife. The surface should be a dark golden brown. Leave for 5-10 minutes before loosening sides and unmoulding on to a serving plate. Serve surrounded with the fresh tomato sauce.

TOMATO SAUCE: Peel the tomatoes and chop them roughly. Add to a pan in which the oil has been heated, with any juice from the tomatoes and the basil or oregano. Simmer for 10-15 minutes, stirring from time to time until the sauce is thick. Purée in a blender or food processor for a smooth sauce or simply remove the basil and season with salt and pepper.

Serves 4-6

Menu 4

Zucchini and Pepper Frittata

A popular Mediterranean vegetable dish which has many variations according to the vegetables used. Cut into wedges to serve.

½ cup finely chopped onion
1½ cups thinly sliced zucchini
¾ cup finely chopped red pepper
¾ cup finely chopped green pepper
salt and freshly ground pepper

2 tablespoons olive oil
8 large eggs
½ cup freshly grated Parmesan
2 tablespoons chopped parsley

In a 23cm (9 inch) frypan cook the onion, zucchini, peppers, with salt and black pepper to taste in 1 tablespoon of the oil over moderate heat. Stir for 10 minutes, or until the vegetables are tender. In a bowl whisk together the eggs, a little salt and pepper to taste, half a cup of the parmesan cheese, the parsley, add the vegetable mixture, and stir the mixture until it is combined well.

In the pan heat the remaining tablespoon oil over moderate heat until it is hot but not smoking, pour in the egg mixture, distributing the vegetables evenly, and cook the frittata, without stirring, for 6 to 8 minutes, or until the edge is set but the centre is still soft. Sprinkle the remaining Parmesan over the top. If the handle is plastic, wrap it in a double thickness of foil. Grill the frittata under a preheated grill for 3 to 4 minutes, or until the cheese is golden. Let it cool in the pan for 5 minutes, and run a knife around the edge. Slide the frittata onto a serving plate, cut it into wedges, and serve warm or at room temperature.

Serves 4-6

A lot of people get peckish between meals. Instead of reaching for a biscuit, try an apple instead.

Menu 4

Strawberry Pignola with Fresh Ricotta

This is one of the best ways to enjoy summer's strawberries — and one that releases all their juices. The pignoli (pine nuts) add their special flavour as well as giving substance to the fruit purée.

2 punnets strawberries
¼ cup pine nuts
1 tablespoon sugar
300g (10oz) ricotta

Put half the strawberries, pine nuts and sugar in a blender and reduce to a smooth, creamy purée. Slice the reserved strawberries. Chill in the refrigerator. Cut ricotta into wedges or use two large dessertspoons to scoop ricotta into rough ovals onto 6 dessert plates. Surround each with the strawberry pignola, finish with fresh strawberries and serve.

Serves 4-6

The Food Combining Menu Cookbook

Basically Good

A few recipes to add to your food combining repertoire. They can be used with a number of menus, and some can be incorporated or substituted into menus.

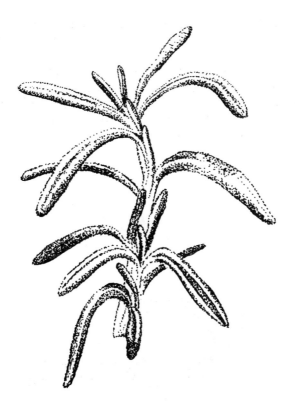

Beef Stock

Protein

Store in plastic bags in the freezer ready for whenever needed. If a brown beef stock is required brown the beef and bones in a hot oven 200°C (400°F) for 30 minutes in a baking dish, turning a few times before adding to the pan with the vegetables and water.

1kg (2lb) shin of beef
2 carrots, sliced
2 leeks or onions, sliced
bouquet garni comprising thyme, bay
  leaf, celery

a little salt and a few peppercorns
1 turnip or a few stalks celery, cut
  into chunks
4 litres (8 pints) water

Wipe the meat with a damp cloth. Place in a large deep saucepan with vegetables. Add seasonings and water to cover. It may be necessary to add more water.

Bring slowly to the boil and remove any scum that forms. Reduce heat, half cover the pan and simmer gently until the flesh has fallen from the bones. This will take 3 hours to extract all the flavour. Cool and strain.

By this time all the goodness has gone from the beef and the vegetables into the stock and so should be discarded.

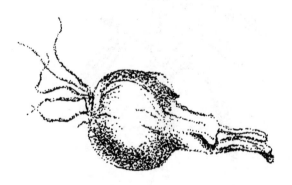

Vegetable Stock

Neutral

Use in place of chicken or beef stock, for both vegetarians and non-vegetarians. Vegetable stock adds a remarkable savor to a dish.

15g (½oz) butter
3 onions, chopped
2 cloves garlic
4 stalks celery with leaves, roughly chopped
3 carrots, roughly chopped
a handful of mushrooms

½ bunch parsley
a bouquet garni comprising a bay leaf, sprig thyme, celery stalk
a little salt to taste and a few peppercorns
5 litres (10 pints) water
1 teaspoon red wine vinegar

Melt the butter in a large heavy pot over a moderate heat. Stir in the onions and sauté for 5 minutes. Add the remaining ingredients except the vinegar. Bring to the boil then reduce the heat to low. simmer, partially covered until reduced and well-flavoured, about 2 hours. Add the vinegar and simmer a further 30 minutes. Strain, gently pressing the liquid out of the vegetables with the back of a spoon.

Use either purified water or bottled, purified water even when you are boiling vegetables and pasta. Pure water is better for your health so drink it regularly between meals.

Chicken Stock

Protein

Make a good flavoursome stock and store in plastic bags in the freezer ready for whenever needed. Chicken bones especially need a little flavour added in the form of giblets, and even though a boiling fowl has plenty of flavour it will be boosted with their addition as well.

1 boiling fowl or 2kg (4lb) chicken
  soup bones
300g (10oz) chicken giblets
2 carrots, sliced
2 leeks or onions, sliced
bouquet garni comprising thyme, bay
  leaf, celery

a little salt and a few peppercorns
1 turnip or a few stalks celery, cut
  into chunks
4 litres (8 pints) water

Place the boiling fowl or chicken soup bones in a large deep saucepan. Add vegetables, seasonings and water to cover. It may be necessary to add more water.

Bring slowly to the boil and remove any scum that forms. Reduce heat, half cover the pan and simmer gently until the flesh is very easily pulled from the boiling fowl. This will take 2-3 hours. Cool and strain.

By this time all the goodness has gone from the boiling fowl and the vegetables into the stock and so should be discarded.

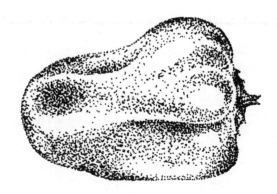

The Food Combining Menu Cookbook

Lentil Soup

Starch

Make this soup with either brown or red lentils. Brown lentils hold their shape while red ones will disintegrate. Both results are good.

2 tablespoons oil
1 onion, chopped
1 carrot, chopped
1 celery stick, chopped
1 clove garlic, crushed
2 teaspoons cumin

⅔ cup brown *or* red lentils
3 cups vegetable stock or water
a little salt and pepper
1 tablespoon chopped parsley to
 garnish, or use coriander leaves
a squeeze of lemon juice

Heat the oil in a large saucepan, add onion, carrot, garlic, celery and cumin, and fry until softened. Add remaining ingredients except parsley and lemon juice, with salt and pepper to taste. Bring to the boil, cover and simmer for 45 minutes, stirring occasionally, then tiny amount of lemon juice. Check the seasoning. Pour into a warmed soup tureen or bowls and sprinkle with parsley or coriander to serve.

Serves 4

Lentil Soup

Starch

1 cup lentils
6 cups water
salt and freshly ground pepper
3 potatoes, peeled and diced

a squeeze lemon juice
2 tablespoons freshly chopped
 parsley or coriander

Put lentils into a large pan with the water, add salt and pepper. Bring to the boil, reduce heat and simmer, covered, for 1½ hours or until lentils are very soft. Add potatoes and simmer for a further 20 minutes until potatoes are tender. Stir in lemon juice and parsley or coriander to serve.

Serves 6

Chawan Mushi

Protein

This is a delicate, savoury egg custard. The secret is to enrich the custard with as much of the stock as possible so that the custard is set, but just barely. Special chawan mushi cups are available wherever Japanese china is sold. Alternatively, conventional heat proof dishes such as small ½-cup size soufflé dishes can be used. It can be eaten with chopsticks or a spoon and can be served piping hot in the traditional way or chilled in the summer months.

100g (3oz) chicken fillet
1 teaspoon light soy sauce
4 small green prawns, shelled and
  deveined (optional)
12 stalks English spinach or
  watercress
4 soaked shitake mushrooms,
  simmered gently for 5 minutes until
  tender
16 ginkgo nuts, shelled and peeled
  (optional)
4 water chestnuts, sliced thinly

CUSTARD:
4 eggs
2½ cups dashi [you can use
  concentrated dashi (about ½ cup to
  2 cups water) or light chicken
  stock]
a pinch of salt
1 tablespoon mirin wine
1 tablespoon light soy sauce

Cut chicken into diagonal slices about 1.5cm (½ inch) long. Marinate in soy sauce for about 15 minutes, then drain. Drop the prawns in a little hot water for about 30 seconds then remove and pat dry. Wash spinach or watercress and chop coarsely. Use ginkgo nuts whole.

CUSTARD: Beat eggs lightly. In another bowl combine the dashi, salt, mirin and light soy sauce. Pour stock gradually into beaten eggs. Mix well without beating, and strain.

Arrange the prepared ingredients between four cups. Spoon the egg mixture into the cups, filling them to about 1.5cm (½ inch) from the top. Cover each cup with foil, place in a steamer and steam gently for 20 minutes, or place in a pan of hot water in a hot oven 220°C (425°F) for 20-30 minutes, until set.

Insert a fine skewer into the centre to test if done. The custard should be just set but still wobble freely.

Note: I make these delicate custards for my family. The children especially like them. I omit the prawns or ginkgo nuts if I don't have them on hand. The custards are still lovely.

Serves 4

The Food Combining Menu Cookbook

Zucchini Frittata

Protein

600g (20oz) zucchini
60g (2oz) pancetta or bacon
2 tablespoons olive oil
a little salt and freshly
  ground pepper

1 tablespoon grated parmesan cheese
6 large eggs, beaten

Top and tail the zucchini and slice. Layer in a colander, sprinkling with salt and leave to drain for 20 minutes or so. Wash and drain thoroughly. Meanwhile cut the pancetta or bacon into lardons and sauté in a heavy frying pan until browned and crisp. Turn into a bowl. Sauté the drained zucchini in the pan with the oil until soft and turn also into the bowl with the pancetta, reserving the oil.

Add the seasonings and cheese and stir in the beaten eggs. Wipe out the pan, return the reserved oil and reheat the pan. Pour egg mixture into heated pan and cook on one side, pulling in the edges a little to allow the uncooked mixture to run underneath. When most of the mixture is cooked, though a little of the top still uncooked, place a flat plate on top to invert the frittata, helping it to turn out with a metal spatula, and using a little patience.

Slide inverted frittata back into pan to cook the top side. Remove from heat while the centre is still soft. Slide out on to a serving plate and serve immediately.

Serves 4-6

Rice with Broad Beans

Starch

Although broad beans are strictly a summer vegetable, the frozen product is excellent. This is a lovely Egyptian way of cooking them, with rice.

3 cups long-grain rice
1kg (2lb) frozen broad beans
Vegetable Stock (see page 119)
30g (1oz) butter *or* 1 tablespoon
  cold-pressed sunflower or oil

salt
4 tablespoon chopped parsley

Wash the rice and drain. Simmer beans in salted boiling water for 2-3 minutes, drain and, if liked, peel the white skin from each bean.

Heat the butter in a pan, add the rice, and stir for a few minutes until the rice becomes transparent. Add salt to taste and enough stock to cover. Bring to the boil and simmer, covered, for about 15 minutes or until the rice is almost tender and the stock has absorbed. Add the beans and simmer a further 5 minutes. Fork the rice and let it rest, still covered, while the remaining moisture is absorbed and the grains become separated. Fork through the parsley and serve.

Rice with Noodles and Peas

Starch

A combination of noodles, rice and peas. Good as a separate dish or serve with a grill.

1 tablespoon light olive oil
1 cup long-grain rice
2 cloves finely chopped garlic
salt and freshly ground pepper
2 tablespoons butter

2 cups vegetable stock
1 cup fine egg noodles, broken
1½ cups shelled or frozen peas
¼ cup finely chopped parsley

Heat the oil in a saucepan and add the rice. Cook, stirring, until well coated. Add the garlic and stir. Add salt and pepper to taste, butter and the stock, bring to the boil, add the noodles and peas. Cover and cook over low heat 16-18 minutes. Stir in the finely chopped parsley and serve.

Serves 4

Nut Cream

Protein

This nut cream is extremely useful as a substitute for cream with a wide range of desserts. It is particularly good for vegetarians.

1 cup cashews
¼ teaspoon vanilla essence
water

In a blender blend all ingredients together, adding water gradually until mixture has formed the texture of thick cream.

Baked Apple and Cheese

Protein

A variation on a cheese board. The cheese becomes warm and it is a lovely combination of crisp and creamy.

2 crisp Granny Smith apples
1 teaspoon tarragon or wine vinegar
4 thick slices chèvre (goat's cheese)
  or 2 small round chèvres

2 teaspoons virgin olive oil
fresh grinding of pepper
sprigs of tender greens or watercress

Cut tops and bottoms from apples then cut in two to make 2 round rings, remove the core and seeds. Brush both cut sides with vinegar. Top each with a slice of chèvre, then season with pepper. Set on ovenproof dish and drizzle with virgin olive oil.

Preheat oven to hot 200°C (400°F), for 5 minutes. Pop into oven and cook for 4 minutes. Watch so that cheese does not run too much. Set on 4 plates and garnish with a few greens.

Index